MINDFUL LEADERSHIP

Learning Through the Practices of Mindfulness and

Compassion

Phe X. Bach, Ed.D.

Table of Contents

Dedication

In loving memory of our Mother, Ai T. Tran and my brother
Thao X. Bach

This book is dedicated to my parents, Long Bach and Ai Tran,
to my wife, Trang Nguyen, and our sons, Khang and Kiet.

Acknowledgements

First, I am appreciative and in gratitude to my wonderful extended family for always believing in me: to my role-model parents, Long Bach and Ai Tran, who are my sources of love and contribution; to my wife, Trang Nguyen, who always was at my side with love, care, and encouragement as well as for giving me our two beautiful sons, Khang and Kiet, who are my motivation, inspiration, and source of labor of love. I value and adore your unconditional love, active caring, and patience.

Second, I would like to acknowledge Dr. W. Edward Bureau for encouraging me to write, as well as for his introduction to this work. Your guidance, support, and friendship are greatly appreciated and valued. I am grateful to Drexel University Sacramento and the involved individuals who have supported the study and research that formed the basis of this book. I am also grateful to know Elizabeth Pema Yangchen as a friend, who helped me with editing. Her meticulousness and passion about the subject enhance the outcome of the messages. Any errors or inconsistencies in the text are solely my responsibility. I also am grateful for Abbess Thích Nữ Thuần Tuệ, who allowed me to help her co-write the mindful leadership training curriculum (The Five Arts of Mindful Leadership) and Quang Tran to translated it into English. I am also appreciate The Most Venerable Thích Nguyên Siêu for let me co-write The Art of Living According to Spiritual Leaders. Furthermore, I appreciate and value Carolyn P. Farias for editing the manuscript.

Lastly, I offer my knowledge and appreciation to the readers, supporters of this book, and practitioners of peace, compassion, altruism, and loving-kindness everywhere.

FOREWORD

Leading From Compassion

Flowing in Dr. Phe Xuan Bach's prose and poetry are notions of intentional mindfulness within ourselves and with others. The universality of Dr. Bach's conceptualization of compassionate, mindful, and peace-based leadership transcends time, nations, and contexts; it can move us toward completeness within ourselves and without with others.

A practicing Buddhist, Dr. Bach weaves the Dharma into both a concept and practice of leadership that transcends the common definitions of it in the West. Deeply he defines and practices "mindful leadership," which is "leading from the inside out." Becoming a mindful leader is nurtured through daily meditation, a practice that grounds us with stillness in which we hear the need for compassion.

Mindful leadership is existential in nature, both timely and timeless. Such is the core of leadership that is being always present in this moment that we share with others. That notion is at the heart of the outreach Phe does to educators throughout California, training them to bring mindfulness into classrooms. Doing so has verifiable mental and physical health benefits for educators and students, but the mindful approach to teaching and learning also creates contexts of compassion and peace.

As leaders, whether in the classroom or elsewhere, we embody what we teach others - the practices of mindfulness. We become examples of mindful leaders who are compassionate, forgiving, and peaceful, embracing the beautiful complexities of ourselves and other human beings. In our moments together we seek harmony that springs from the wells of empathy and of suspending judgment about each other.

Leading ourselves and others through change, metaphorically, is the water in the river flowing around the rocks, always moving, always flowing. We learn to embrace change and let go of what we cannot control. As mindful leaders, our daily practice helps us find a constancy in the milieu of change and peace in helping others navigate what would seem to be troubling waters.

Flowing beneath and throughout Phe's poems and prose are soothing currents of letting go, of reassurance that mindfulness and compassion can nurture sustainable peace within ourselves and others. May Phe's writings give us a pause for reflection and transformation.

W. Edward Bureau, PhD

Cochranville, Pennsylvania

May 2019

Leading by Example Leadership

(A leadership poem resulting from my own meditation and reflecting upon spiritual leadership)

Leadership,

any leadership model must have guidelines.

Set solid principles and objectives,

then create the standard of excellence.

Leading by Example

is the foundation of life and leadership,

for others to follow

and inspire,

to have a shared, common vision, with abundant enthusiasm and action.

There are many different paths to our ultimate goals,

but these roads must be built on

the foundation of compassion, wisdom, and courage.

We must envision the future, create a practical ideal,

consider the potential uniqueness of the organization, persuade and take

quiet action for all to see and follow.

An exciting and wonderful future

We must take the challenge,

and look for innovative ways

to improve our organization.

Experiment, take risks,

and learn from the mistakes and failures.

They present opportunities for growth

and transformation.

For a better future

we must take action,

promote and support each other.

Cooperation and collaboration for sustainable change. Positivity,

mutual respect, and unity

are all so precious,

like the rhythm of the heart.

Extraordinary effort,

inner values and human dignity

are the key,

My dear mindfulness-practitioner friends.

Hard work is ahead,

our hopes and dreams

will come true

when we live for the greater good,

and when we contribute to the development of humanity with great understanding and love, tolerance and forgiveness.

CHAPTER 1

A FOUNDATION OF MINDFUL
LEADERSHIP

CHANGE: FEAR ME NOT – EMBRACE ME

Five thoughts on fostering change

M

ost people are resistant to change. This is true for any society and for people from all walks of life. Change requires a lot of effort, commitment, and energy; therefore, we often prefer the path of least resistance. We enjoy being in our comfort zones, and tend to fear change, because it brings uncertainty and leads us into the unknown. Perhaps the greatest fear of all is the fear of the unknown. Fear is natural, but if we recognize and embrace it, we can transform it into something positive and productive.

Like hatred and prejudice, fear is a very strong emotion, thus it can produce an enormous amount of energy. That energy can be very destructive. We need to pause, reflect, and recognize it. In doing so, we will see that the cause of fear is not knowing. The people who fear change the most, often feel insecure, unprepared, and inadequate to conquer new endeavors. Sometimes, change makes them feel like victims and out of control. But in reality, we are in full control of our response.

While we can't control anyone else's thoughts, speech, actions, or emotions, we can control our own. Controlling our own thoughts, speech, actions, and emotions is the first step in facing change. Once we recognize and face change with mindfulness, we can embrace and transform it. Here are five thoughts that can foster our acceptance of change.

1. Lay a foundation of compassion and love with a moral purpose.

2. Control your own emotions and well-being.

3. Be sincere with regard to your intention and mission.

4. Have confidence in your own abilities and flexibility.

5. Harvest the labor of love and be proud of the work you do.

Nurturing change is the process of planting the seeds of compassion for the greater good. To put it succinctly, change is a natural process and it is like a weed-- it is easy to grow and to react negatively to it. But it takes a lot of time and love to mold something unpleasant into something beautiful like a bonsai. Changes present a great opportunity for fulfillment. When we challenge ourselves, there is great potential for the end result to be extremely satisfying and beneficial for all. So, why be fearful? Life is a constant process of change—it's impermanent. Embrace and enjoy the beauty of it.

Mindful Leadership - Five Arts of Leadership For Buddhist Youth Leaders: With An Emphasis on Awareness Practice

Abbess Thích Nữ Thuần Tuệ and Tâm Thường Định

Right Mindfulness, *Sammà sati* in Pali, means to think positive thoughts, to be enlightened in that moment, and to comprehend all Dharma completely. Mindfulness is an integral part of the Noble Eightfold Path—the eight methods of the path to peace and liberation—within the fourth Noble Truth.

According to Theravada Buddhist tradition, mindfulness is the heart of meditation and conscious awareness of all phenomena that arise in the present moment. In other words, mindfulness is to know what is currently occurring. Mindfulness is the energy that originates from self-observation of what is going on internally and externally. Mindfulness brings us back to the present moment since the present is a beautiful gift that we can treasure here and now.

In accordance with Buddhist tradition, mindfulness is essential to the development of Right Concentration *(Sammà samadhi)*, the method used to receive and maintain moral conducts in life. Mindfulness has many functions. The first one is to recognize everything that is occurring presently. The second function is awareness of thoughts that arise in our mind. Gradually, mindfulness guides practitioners to Right Concentration, and, ultimately, Perfect Wisdom.

Leadership, by our definition, is to guide others in the spirit of giving without expecting any reciprocation, and helping ourselves along with others indiscriminately. Normally, a good leader possesses the following three traits:

1.   *Have a benevolent vision and the capability to positively inspire and influence others in mindfulness.*

2.   *Advocate and transmit that ideal vision to fellow practitioners and oneself via his/her practice of mindfulness.*

3.   *Instill joy, benefit, and peace to oneself and others at this very moment and future moments.*

Mindful leadership allows "the leader" to transcend the boundaries of time and space in order to bring peace to everyone. This transcendence is only possible if the leaders' thoughts, speech and actions stem from altruism and compassion. In this spirit, we would like to share this topic on Mindful Leadership to the leaders of the Vietnamese Buddhist Youth Association *(Gia Đình Phật Tử)* in particular and all beings as a whole.

The art of mindful leadership consists of five main points:

1.   Deep listening and empathy

2.   Sound judgment

3.   Living in harmony with others

4.   Teaching through actions

5.   A kind heart

We will begin with the word *"Huynh Trưởng,"* which means an older brother, an older sister, or someone with experiences whose responsibility is to protect and guide younger members *(đàn em)*. A role model Huynh Trưởng needs to be calm, caring, tolerant, and sound in order to fulfill their aforementioned tasks. A Huynh Trưởng is an active member with duties and responsibilities toward the VBYA. A Huynh Trưởng guides and nurtures younger members while accepting and fulfilling tasks/activities to sustain and grow the VBYA local chapter *(đơn vị)*. Lastly, a Huynh Trưởng is an excellent citizen and contributes constructively to society. Leadership is an art filled with dedication. Here is a classic example:

Long ago, the president lectured about leadership at a United States Military Academy. He took out a bundle of rope from his pocket and placed it on a table. He challenged students to push the rope across the table; many students attempted this task, but they all struggled to push the rope across the table. As they pushed, the rope would curl, twist or tangle; it was an impossible task!

After all students conceded, the president laughed kindly and slowly rearranged the rope back to its original position. Next, with his thumb and index finger, he pulled the rope along the table. The remaining rope followed his hand and glided across the table effortlessly. The president explained, *"People are like a bundle of rope. If we lead them, they will follow. But if we push them, they will push back, creating unwanted complications."*

To be capable leaders, we need to practice, understand, and apply teachings like the Five Vidyas (*Ngũ Minh*) and Three Teaching Methods (*Thân Giáo, Khẩu Giáo, Ý Giáo*). Remember, a person that does not know direction cannot navigate another person and a person without money cannot donate money to anyone. Likewise, a leader cannot share knowledge and skills that they are not comfortable explaining in detail. In order to teach and guide younger members, a leader first needs to be trained accordingly.

Generally, everyone wants to be a good, admirable, and kind person, but flaws and bad habits are difficult to hide. Gradually, young members will learn to not trust a leader with glaring flaws, noticeable bad habits, and lackadaisical efforts. A leader can try to hide his/her shortcomings; however, the truth cannot stay hidden forever.

Practicing mindfulness allows leaders to rapidly improve themselves. Normally, the mind constantly wanders every day, everywhere; and therefore, mindfulness reminds the mind to return to the present. Mindfulness brings the mind home. Mindfulness grants the practitioner the ability to be in true contact with the people and situations at hand. Intangible - mindfulness cannot exist in the form of thoughts but can be perceived by keen hearts.

Below are details associated with the Art of Mindfulness.

I. DEEP LISTENING AND EMPATHY

1. Be Silent

Please listen to the whole sentence. Please do not respond immediately. Please do not jump to conclusions. Please be empathetic to others' difficulties.

I like to share this short Zen anecdote titled *"Say and Listen"* from Zen Master Gettan *(Nguyệt Am)*. The Zen Master frequently reminded his students that *"When you use your mouth to speak, your ears are not listening. When you use your ears to listen, your mouth is not speaking. Please contemplate this notion."*

2. Be empathetic

Life often has two facets: an obvious facet and a more subtle one. Here is another example:

Not too long ago in Vietnam, a neighbor complained to his elderly friend:

"The neighboring house just bought a karaoke machine. My God! The little girl sang like a moaning cow. And the son... He roared like a tiger. I have headaches listening to them. "

The elder friend calmly replied, "I feel the same way. But those kids are not out drinking alcohol, stealing from villagers, or harming the village. Those actions are more troublesome; therefore, we must be more tolerant for the village's safety."

Below is another example:

It was afternoon and kids were asleep in the nursery. John was thirsty and went to Miss Roberts'. He whispered, *"May I have some water?"*

Half-asleep, Miss Roberts awoke grumpily and unpleasantly answered, *"Allowed."*

"Miss Roberts, may I have some water?" John asked again. This time his voice was a bit louder.

Annoyed that John was asking again, she responded with a loud, *"Allowed."*

"Miss Roberts, may I have some water?" John asked the same question for the third time. This time his voice was very loud.

"Allowed." Miss Roberts yelled her answer.

"MISS ROBERTS! MAY I HAVE SOME WATER?" John scream with all his might, waking up all the sleeping children. Angered, Miss Roberts lost her temper and yelled, *"John! Are you messing with me?"*

Scared and confused, John answered, puzzled, *"No, Miss Roberts. You told me to say aloud!"*

What happened in this comical short story? Why did John misunderstand Miss Roberts' words? When Miss Roberts answered with *"allowed,"* John misheard and thought Miss Roberts said *"aloud."* This is an example of homophones; words that sound similar but have different meanings. To distinguish between homophones, we use context, but John has yet to learn about homophones and reacted inappropriately. Miss Roberts overlooked the situation and wrongly assumed John was playing a game.

In general, a leader needs to remember:

- Do not control others.

- Do not expect others to see your viewpoints.

- Do not depend on others for happiness.

President Abraham Lincoln famously said, *"I destroy my greatest enemies when I make them my friends."* Similarly, a leader needs to focus on the positive aspects of his team possesses rather than the weaknesses within the team.

3. Sharing is leadership

Please use this story about changing people's lives as an example:

In the year 1921, Lewis Lawes served as warden for the Sing Sing Correctional Facility, a prison known for its harsh conditions. Twenty years later, upon his retirement, this prison had transformed into a humane site. When asked about these remarkable transformations, Lawes credited his wife, Kathryn, for instilling these changes.

Even before her first visit to the Sing Sing Correctional Facility, Kathryn heard many rumors about this dreadful place and its prisoners. Her first visit to the prison was during its first basketball game held between prisoners. Kathryn sat and watched with her children among prisoners. She felt neither fear nor repulsiveness. She believed these prisoners would treat her well since she and her husband treated them well.

When she saw a blind man that was convicted with murder, she held his hands and tenderly asked whether he knew Braille. He did not. She taught him how to read. Upon meeting prisoners that were mute and deaf, she learned and taught sign language to them. From 1921 to 1937, prisoners within the Sing Sing Correctional Facility viewed Kathryn as a living saint, an angel.

When Kathryn died from a car accident, Lewis Lawes took leave to oversee his wife's funeral. The vice-warden saw how these so-called cruel prisoners gathered in front of the main gate; their faces were filled with tears. He knew how much they loved and appreciated Kathryn. Thus, he allowed them to leave the facility without any supervision from guards as long as they returned by nighttime. All prisoners walked over a kilometer of distance to attend Kathryn's funeral and returned to Sing Sing on time as promised.

4. *Avoid jumping to conclusions*

The act of judging a person is actually the mind trying to manifest itself. To better ourselves, we should stop judging others.

a. Please use this short story as an example. One day, the father brought home a beautiful bird inside a cage; he hung the cage on a tree in the garden. The mother also brought home a cute cat, which could roam freely. A few days later, the father returned home and did not see his prized bird; meanwhile, the cat was sunbathing in the garden. The father blamed the cat for eating his precious bird while the mother fervently defended her cat. They quarreled non-stop. Angered, the father left the house for work while the mother went back to her parent's house, carrying the youngest child. Later that night, the neighbor brought over the lost bird, which flew out of his opened cage, but no one was home except for the servants.

b. This famous story called *"Nhan Hồi and the rice pot"* is another beautiful example. During the Eastern Zhou time period of Ancient China's history, Confucius led a pilgrimage from Lo, his homeland, to Qi, a thriving city-state. Among his many distinguished students, Nhan Hồi *(Yan Hui)* and Tử Lộ *(Min Sun)* were the most recognized and favorite ones. At that time, wars between neighboring city-states were frequent and long-lasting. People struggled for survival; starvation and misery were common everywhere. Confucius and his students also suffered the same fate. On their journey, they starved for many days; their meals consisted simply of vegetables and porridge. Despite these rigorous and extreme conditions, all students followed their teacher's journey with determination. Fortunately, upon reaching Qi, a merchant recognized Confucius and donated rice to the group. Confucius entrusted Tử Lộ to his remaining students in search for vegetables in the forest. Meanwhile, Nhan Hồi was designated the task of cooking rice. Nhan Hồi was given this crucial and important task since he was a virtuous person, for whom Confucius had trust and high expectations.

Nhan Hồi began cooking the rice as the group led by Tử Lộ left to find vegetables. Meanwhile, facing the kitchen, Confucius was reading old doctrines. Suddenly, Confucius heard a loud noise emerging from the kitchen. He looked toward the kitchen to see Nhan Hồi opening the rice pot's lid, stirring the cooked rice with chopsticks. Once finished, glancing around, Nhan Hồi slowly ate the rice.

Confucius witnessed all of Nhan Hồi's actions and sighed to the Heaven in disappointment, "Oh! My best student! He ate before his teacher and friends… What a scoundrel! How could all my expectations suddenly disappear into thin air…"

A moment later, Tử Lộ returned with vegetables, which Nhan Hồi steamed in boiling water. In misery, Confucius continued to remain in silence. When the vegetables were cooked, Nhan Hồi and Tử Lộ prepared the table for dinner. Once everything was ready, all students gathered to invite Confucius for dinner. Looking at his students, Confucius said, "My students. The journey from Lo to Qi was long and tiresome. I am pleased that you remain pure at heart, continue to love and protect each other, and follow my teachings despite harsh and starving conditions. Today, our first day in Qi, we are blessed with a warm meal. This first meal in Qi reminds me of my homeland, Lo. I remember my parents. I want to offer a bowl of rice to my parents. May I?"

All students except Nhan Hồi folded their hands and answered, "Yes!"

Confucius continued, "I want to ensure that this rice is pure first."

Confused, his students glanced around for an answer. At that moment, Nhan Hồi folded his hands and answered, "My dear teacher, this rice is not pure."

Confucius asked, "Why?"

Nhan Hồi answered, "When I opened the lid to check whether the rice had evenly cooked, a gust of wind blew by causing soot and dust to fall into the rice. I tried to stop these debris from soiling the rice but I could not block them all. I immediately removed the soiled rice and was about to discard them, but then I thought: We have a lot of people, but we are short on rice. If I discard these soiled rice, we will be short a serving portion of rice, and everyone will eat less. Therefore, I dared to eat the soiled rice beforehand. I dedicate these clean rice to you, my teacher, and my friends.

"Dear teacher! I have already eaten my portion of rice for today. Please excuse me from eating rice this meal. I will just eat vegetables. And lastly, we should not offer rice that has been eaten as a worship."

After hearing Nhan Hồi's response, Confucius looked up to the Heaven and exclaimed, "Alas! There are things in this world that you clearly see but still cannot comprehend the truth. I almost became a fool!"

II. SOUND JUDGMENT

A leader needs to be a role model and an embodiment for wisdom in order to safely guide and benefit followers. When our mind resides in mindfulness, our mind is not lost in thoughts and is in true contact with the present situation. This mental state allows us to find the best solution to any given problem.

Consider this short story. A group of merchants traveled under the hot sun without an adequate supply of water. Upon entering a new village, the group saw a huge tree full of ripe, juicy fruits. The group yelled in excitement and began climbing the tree. Suddenly, the leader stopped everyone:

"My friends. You should not eat these fruits. If these fruits were indeed edible, villagers and other travelers would have eaten them already. Since these fruits have not been eaten, these fruits are poisonous."

Listening to the leader's sound judgment, the group continued forward.

Another group of merchants arrived at the exact same location shortly. Everyone in the group quickly devoured these fruits. As expected, these fruits contained toxins, and the whole group was poisoned. In this instance, the leader lacked the needed wisdom to guide and protect his group to safety.

The Buddha taught us:

1. *Address the problem promptly and facilitate discussion. Be aware that unhappy people do not like to be lectured. Remember the story regarding Gotami and her dead child. The Buddha did not lecture Gotami but instructed her to seek a family that had not experienced death. Gotami eventually realized the truth regarding death.*

2. *State the facts. Avoid explanations and accusations based on self-analysis or self-speculation. Avoid exaggerations and elaborations.*

3. *Use neutral words that are not biased.*

4. *Speak with an intention of benefitting the audience. Focus on positive aspects within the situation. Avoid criticisms that lead to arguments.*

5. *Speak from compassion, not from anger.*

Furthermore, The Buddha also emphasized: "Sariputta, although you have followed these five methods of dialogue, there are people that still will not change. This is due to pre-conceived notions (sở tri chướng) within them."

III. LIVING IN HARMONY WITH OTHERS

1. Recognize our ego

Mindfulness and ego cannot and will not coexist. Ego intrinsically causes confrontation and disagreement since ego has the tendency to want to be correct, to be the best, to be the alpha, to be number one. Everyone has this ego. Whenever our ego feels superior, we react boastfully; whenever our ego feels inferior, we react aggressively. To protect and strengthen itself, each individual ego clashes with other egos, creating conflicts. Sadly, we fail to recognize that we are inadvertently hurting others as we satisfy our ego.

To live in harmony, our ego needs to be lowered and we must be more accepting. We should live with this motto: ***respect our superiors, love our inferiors, and tolerate our equals.***

2. Right and wrong

Never be one-hundred percent certain that you are correct, for being correct leads to arguments and conflicts. Our definition of correct only applies to ourselves; as a result, others probably have different viewpoints and will not accept our point-of-views. Being less certain causes less controversy, conflict, and anger from happening.

If we respect the viewpoints of others and acknowledge others' logic, we can live and work in harmony for eternity.

Phe X. Bach, Ed.D.

Venerable Zen Master Thích Thanh Từ once said, *"We often have a tendency to believe our thoughts are absolute truth. Thus, our thoughts and others' thoughts clash, leading to arguments, anger, and violence."*

Venerable Thích Thanh Từ reflected, *"When I was living in the mountain, I saw rain clouds approaching my direction from afar. I wholeheartedly believed that rain was coming, so I quickly moved everything inside. However, the wind would change the clouds direction, leading to no rain. Therefore, our thoughts are never one-hundred percent correct. We tend to think we are correct; our assumption gives rise to conflict and disagreement."*

In the Sutra, the Buddha taught, *"One who respects the truth would say 'This is my thought' and would stop talking. If one says my thought is correct, one is no longer respecting the truth. Adding the word 'right' creates controversy."*

3. Be calm and happy

Never view anything as absolute importance. Be optimistic and have a positive outlook. Acknowledge praiseworthy characteristics and behaviors within the people we are interacting with or the present situation. Cherish what we presently have. Do not expect everything to go according to our expectations. If we live according to principles mentioned above, our mind will be at peace. Our personal practice will generate positive energy that benefits the collective community.

IV. TEACHING THROUGH ACTIONS

In the article *"Thân Giáo: Có thể là một giải pháp cho tất cả"*, I emphasize that Buddhism is based on the principles of compassion and wisdom, cultivated through personal practice. Teaching through actions is a valuable and practical lesson that the Buddha taught since we can easily apply this practice to daily life in multiple instances. The evolution in international peace can be traced to the Buddha's teachings. Nowaday, Buddhism remains a solution to most modern problems within society. As the author, I raise the following seven points:

1.   Establish a humane mindset

2.   Comprehend cause and effect with karma

3.   Improve our surroundings

4.   Practice mutual respect and mutual benefit

5.   Be there to assist others

6.   Remember strength in numbers

7.   Be a Buddhist practitioner

In general, a leader needs to earn others' trust and cooperate with others in the spirit of compassion and altruism. This is only possible when a leader possesses both respect and affection toward others. A reliable leader is someone younger members can depend on and learn from in multiple situations.

- One should acts as one teaches others

- Only with oneself through thoroughly tamed should one tame others

- To tame oneself is, indeed, difficult.

- -Excerpted from Verse 159 of the Dhammapada

Our actions reflect the degree of our personal practices, which are based on precepts, perseverance, and diligence. With compassion and vows to benefit others, the Buddha attained enlightenment to guide and save people from suffering.

1. *Practice mindfulness*

Be conscious of your actions. Unite the mind and body. For example:

a. While walking, be aware of which foot you are moving. Be aware of each movement you make within the day.

b. Mindfulness can prevent mental illness like Alzheimer's disease. Remember forgetfulness and unawareness hinder the accomplishment of goals.

2. *Practice awareness*

a. Be aware of the 6 senses. Know the present clearly and uninterruptedly.

b. Realize when our mind drifts toward self-attachment and unkind thoughts.

c. Live in the present. Relax body and mind.

3. *Wisdom and compassion are the two doors that lead to liberation.*

4. *Lead ourselves*

In order to lead, a leader must have high self-esteem and peoples' trust. People trust and listen to a leader because that leader is caring and devoted not because that leader possesses power.

5. *Flagrance diffuses from the flower*

Cultivate spiritual energy through personal practices. Share that cultivated energy with the collective.

6. *Results do not fall from the sky.*

Genius cultivates good habits that are accumulated from previous lives or decades of intense hard work and dedication.

V. A KIND HEART

A good leader consistently reflects on whether understanding, love, and unity are more important than being right.

Years ago, a Hindu follower undertook a pilgrimage toward a holy temple within the Himalayan mountains. The road was long, steep, and windy; the condition was hot and oxygen level was low due to the elevation. Despite carrying little to no supply, he hiked vexingly while breathing heavily. Oftentimes, he stopped to rest while wishing his destination would appear before him. Suddenly he saw a young girl about 10-years-old walking toward him. Gasping for breath and sweating profusely, she was piggybacking a small child with all her might.

The Hindu follower approached the young girl and sympathetically spoke, *"My dear child. You must be as tired as me. You carry a heavy load!"*

The girl corrected, *"What you carry is weight. What I carry is my brother, not weight."*

The follower's load feels heavy because he does not possess love. Love provides us with the strength to face adversities with ease. Life is meaningful when we live with true love and aim toward clear ideals.

Love requires sacrifice. Without love, a sacrifice will definitely feel like a burden. This world will become more beautiful if everyone shares responsibilities and obligations that benefit the collective, including family, community, and religion.

Everyone lives a meaningful life while shouldering a very gentle burden together and sharing fraternal love as we aspire toward that common, lofty goal.

From these short vignettes, I summarize the main points in the following poem:

Mindful Leadership

- Deep listening and sympathy

- Calm in all instances

- Harmony from accordance

- Sound and wise decisions

- No anger, ignorance, flattery

- Hone the Four Assistant Methods (Tứ Nhiếp Pháp)

- Maintain a pure mind

- Define Mindful Leadership

CONCLUSION

Nowadays, technology and science continue to advance at a rate that far exceeds that of spiritual development. Whether we are monastics or lay followers, leaders or young members of the VBYA organization, male or female, young or old, members or not members of VBYA—as Buddhists, we need to practice and apply Buddhism with solemnity to transform ourselves and surroundings. We need to mend our flaws and bad habits to gradually better ourselves. In addition, we need to fulfill our duties and obligations whenever and wherever possible with fervor. Accepting our roles, duties, and responsibilities as a VBYA leader with utmost genuineness, we practice mindfulness to radiate the energy of compassion and wisdom. These spiritual energies will nourish and strengthen our younger members. That is the essence of mindful leadership. Dear friends, let's commence our journey.

Translated by Quang Tran

THE ART OF LIVING ACCORDING TO SPIRITUAL LEADERS

Phe Bach, Ed.D.

Kim Quang Buddhist Temple and Drexel University Sacramento

Most Venerable Thich-Nguyen-Sieu

Phật Đà Buddhist Temple of San Diego, CA.

W. Edward Bureau, Ph.D.

Drexel University.

Abstracts:

Leaders, in any institution, may have many virtues and spirituality qualities. As spiritual leaders, one must live peaceful and harmonious live in accordance with our family, community, society, and homeland. They often have strong relationships with others and have strong inner values such as selflessness and harmony. Spiritual leaders also must have a lofty spirit and morals. Some of these moral values include compassion, diligence, determination, joy, gratitude, love, integrity, honesty, mindfulness, perseverance, responsibility, trustworthiness, understanding and wisdom. This paper, through examining our psychological experiences, as well as our personally lived experiences in our own lives, suggests the five arts of living. They are:

1) The First Art Of Living Is To Live As Bamboo Trees;

2) The Second Art Of Living Is To Live As A River;

3) The Third Art Of Living Is To Live As the *Mai* Tree;

4) The Fourth Art Of Living Is To Live As Earth; and

5) The Fifth Art Of Living Is To Live As The Clouds.

These five core principles frame specific practices and directions for everyone, Buddhists and non-Buddhists alike—including spiritual leaders, laypersons, and the Sangha—who wish that individuals, families, and societies be more harmonious, more peaceful and more happy.

Leaders and spirituality

Boorom (2009) suggested that leadership has roots in religion, as there is a direct correlation between leadership and spiritual qualities. Marques (2010) suggests that "it is perfectly possible to be spiritual yet not religious. There are many spiritual people who are atheists, agnostics, or that embrace multiple religions at the same time" (p.13). For her, "a spiritual worker is a person who simply maintains good human values, such as respect, tolerance, goodwill, support, and an effort to establish more meaning in his or her workplace" (p. 13). DeVost (2010) emphasized that current research in organizations has found a relationship between the spirituality of the leaders and the spirituality in the workplace. In this study, Devost (2010) found that the practice of 'encouraging the heart" – one of the five exemplified leadership values -- was significantly positive. According to Kouzes & Posner

(1995), the five practices of good leadership are: "challenge the process, inspire a shared vision, enable others to act, model the way, and encourage the heart" (p. 9).

Meanwhile, leaders often put their spiritual lives into practice, as well as their moral beliefs and ethical values. As Northouse (2004) has argued, ethics and leadership are "concerned with the kinds of values and morals an individual or society finds desirable or appropriate" (p. 342). Furthermore, he pointed out that an ethical model of leadership consists of five components: a) showing respect, b) serving others, c) showing justice, d) manifesting honesty and e) building community. In another study, Zhu, May, & Avolio (2004) define ethical leadership as "doing what is right, just and good" (p. 16). Zhu et al. (2004) added that leaders exhibit ethical behaviors when they are doing what is morally right, just, and good, and when they help to elevate followers' moral awareness and moral self-actualization. Bass and Steidlmeier (1998) suggest that a truly transformational and effective leadership must be based upon: a) the moral character of the leader and his or her concern for oneself and others, b) the ethical values embedded in the leader's vision, and c) the morality of the processes and social ethical choices and actions in which the leaders and followers engage.

The art of living life is about how we live peacefully with ourselves in accordance with our family, community, society, and homeland. As men and women laity (laypersons), we must live to obtain harmony, peace and happiness for ourselves. Reading from the classic Sutras (teachings of the Buddha) and through examining our psychological experiences, as well as our personally lived experiences in our own lives, we can see the virtues of the bamboo, the rivers, the apricot (mai) trees, the earth, and the clouds. From there, we can extract the art of living a Buddhist life.

The First Art Of Living Is To Live As Bamboo Trees

We can see and understand the humble beauty and flexibility of the bamboo trees—when a gust of wind blows through the bamboo, it, being flexible, will be swept with the direction of the wind. This phenomenon illustrates how life moves and bends under different conditions, and how we need to live responding according to the elements for things to coexist. We ought to understand ourselves as well as others around us. We must nurture our true self—the core values within—therefore, when we make contact with difficult real-life situations we are not broken, nor do we feel like we have lost a part of ourselves. Flexibility is a characteristic of the bamboo trees: they never fall apart within a storm. They move within the storm, yielding to that which will leave them standing, without breaking. As laypeople, when we are faced with problems in life, we need to be flexible like the bamboo. We need to build within ourselves the art of living with others in different situations and circumstances.

The Second Art Of Living Is To Live As A River

The spirit of Buddhism is both formlessness and *Tùy Duyên* (Sanskrit: *Pratitysamutpad*--dependent arising). The spirit of Buddhism is not a fixed character nor a phenomenon that is subjective and always a rigid status quo.

The spirit of Buddhism depends on conditions. So the spirit of the Buddhist precepts (or spiritual discipline) is not rigid. It depends on conditions and circumstances; it is not fixed. Therefore, in the path of propagating Dharma transmission in a new land, to a different ethnicity or culture, Buddhism always flows as is appropriate and its transmission is dissolved into the new ethnic culture.

For over 2600 years, the presence of Buddhism in this world has eased pain and suffering. There is no trace of blood or tears in the name of "Dharma Transmission" in Buddhism. That is because of the spirit of *Tùy Duyên* (dependent arising) in Buddhism. Therefore, we need to adopt the art of living as a river: water flows from upstream to downstream and out to sea. If a river lies on a high plateau, the water flows quickly downstream, but when the river is down below the plateau, the water flows gently; slowly, more poetically, and then the river merges and integrates into the sea without holding a fixed nature.

In life, too, living in our environment or facing certain circumstances, we have to apply the art of dissolving (in life with everyone, with other sentient beings, and with the social environment) without holding on to our self-centered egos. The reason that we have to suffer or face dissatisfaction is because of our egos. We refuse to let it go; we want to cling to our ego or we are simply not willing to dissolve it with the masses of people. We identify with our ego and superego as our beings; and when we pay attention to our ego, it gets bigger. Thus, we think that we are the most important individuals and that others must listen to us. We tend to forget that in this life, all sentient beings have Buddha Nature.

We all have access to the knowledge and practices, as well as the potential to be awakened. So, we have to respect each other. From an old man to a child, we must always remain in harmony, courteous, humble, and compassionate towards each other, according to the precepts. If our ego is too big, it will create a big wobble and topple our lives. The ego will never put our life at ease or make it peaceful. As laypersons, we need to eliminate or let go of our dogmatic views and ego. Every day we need to work at reducing our egos; the more we let go, the more harmony we will have with others. In the language of the Sutras, the art of living as a river is the ability to dissolve into the ocean. River water cannot retain its personal, or ego-identified, identity of the river, but has to merge and integrate into the vast ocean. Both the river and the ocean are referred to as water. Water dissolves in water and so should our own selves with others.

The Third Art Of Living Is To Live As the *Mai* Tree

The *mai* is a unique tree in Vietnam. It is known as a great tree due to its longevity. With its bulky and rough bark, at first sight, we understand at once it must be able to undergo many hardships: rain or shine, season to season. The roots of the *mai* tree are firmly grounded in the hillside supporting the tree to stand on its own and exist in this universe. All kinds of weather conditions have coated its stems and roots, yet the *mai* tree still reaches out and progresses with endurance through time—rain or shine—until a day in springtime, when *mai* flowers bloom with beauty and fragrance.

The *mai* is the symbol for patience and optimism. It faces weather and obstacles and yet it will blooms and displays its beauty, although time may wreak havoc. People, too, are always changing and aging—we are born, we grow up, and eventually pass away. From observing and understanding the *mai* tree, the layperson can cultivate Buddha-hood. This does not happen within a short period of time, but through many rebirths, many lives crossing the rapid currents of suffering, life and death. Thus we have to train our mind with determination to attain Buddha-hood. We can practice the teachings of the Buddha and affirm our mind and heart in the Dharma Realm, similar to how the *mai* tree patiently endures the rain, the sun, or the storm. Thus, when we are facing challenges, difficulties, or hardships in life, we must overcome them, careful to keep our mindfulness, and not flinch, nor break our will in order to achieve success on the path to enlightenment through our own practices.

The Fourth Art Of Living Is To Live As Earth

Being patient, enduring, robust, and forgiving, the earth produces and raises all things in the world. Humans live well on this planet because of the earth. We live and pass on this land and so does everything else. Therefore, the earth symbolizes the virtue of fortitude and endurance. When we irrigate the earth with polluted waters, it does not reject or complain; likewise when we irrigate it with clean water, the earth does not rejoice or become excited.

On the path of our own practice, we need to learn from the earth: that is an art of living. By doing so, we will have peace and equanimity in this chaos of life. If we become unbalanced in our lives, unlike the earth, we are dependent on the sound of praise and criticism, and thus we suffer dis-ease or experience dissatisfaction. If we are pleased with praise or displeased with criticism, then we are living by others' desires, and that means that we have not mastered ourselves. So, we have to live patiently and endure as does the earth.

The Fifth Art Of Living Is To Live As The Clouds

Clouds are floating. The art of living here is to be free and not encumbered. The clouds do not stay still, they travel and dispatch in all directions. They are neither stuck in one place nor contaminated by other factors. Buddhists should keep their hearts and minds free, open, and unattached to phenomena. If our heart and mind are attached and not open, this causes hindrances and obstacles to appear, which make it hard to reach enlightenment. When our minds are filled with greed, hatred, and ignorance or stuck by praise-criticism, love-hate, satisfaction-dissatisfaction, then our minds are not as free-floating as the clouds. So, we need to live like the clouds, which is the fifth art of living. Be free--selfless and at ease, floating freely without attachments.

The above is a quick summary of the five arts of living. As spiritual leaders, one must have strong relationships with others and have strong inner values such as selflessness and harmony. Spiritual leaders also must have a lofty spirit and morals. Some of these moral values include compassion, diligence, determination, joy, gratitude, love, integrity, honesty, mindfulness, perseverance, responsibility, trustworthiness, understanding and wisdom (Bach, 2014). We pray for and encourage all of us to know how to live an artful life: to be as flexible and humble as the bamboo trees, as integrating and dissolving as the river, as enduring and optimistic as the *mai* tree, as patient and forgiving as the earth, and as selfless and free as clouds. These five core principles frame specific practices and directions for everyone (including spiritual leaders, laypersons, and the Sangha) who wishes that individuals, families, and societies be more harmonious, more peaceful and happier.

References:

Bach, P. X. (2014). Mindful Leadership–A Phenomenological Study of Vietnamese Buddhist Monks in America with Respect to their Spiritual Leadership Roles and Contributions to Society (Doctoral dissertation, Drexel University).

Bass, B. M., & Steidlmeier, P. (1998). Ethics, character, and authentic transformational leadership. http://cls.binghamton.edu/bassSteid.html

Boorom, R. (2009). "Spiritual leadership: A study of the relationship between spiritual leadership theory and transformational leadership". Regent University. ProQuest Dissertations and Theses,175-n/a. Retrieved from http://search.proquest.com/docview/305133283?accountid=10559. (305133283).

DeVost, R. (2010). Correlation between the leadership practices of lead ministers and the workplace spirituality of their churches as reported by church members. Andrews University). ProQuest Dissertations and Theses,

Retrieved from

http://search.proquest.com/docview/871103857?accounti

d=10559

Kouzes, J. M. & Posner, B. Z. (1995). The leadership change: How to keep getting extraordinary things done in organization. San Francisco: Jossey-Bass.

Marques, J. (2010). Spirituality, meaning, interbeing, leadership, and empathy: SMILE. Interbeing, 4(2), 7.

Northouse, P. (2004). Leadership theory and practice (3rd ed.). Thousand Oaks, CA: Sage Publication

Zhu, W., May, D.R., & Avolio, B.J. (2004). "The impact of ethical leadership behavior on employee outcomes: The roles of psychological empowerment and authenticity." Journal of Leadership & Organizational Studies, 11(1), 16.

Mindful Leadership

Leadership at The Vietnamese

Buddhist Youth Association (VBYA)

This research paper examines the leadership at The Vietnamese Buddhist Youth Association (VBYA), also known as *Gia Dinh Phat Tu* (GDPT) in Vietnamese, a non-profit organization that emphasizes not only on virtue (moral, ethical, and inner values) but also focuses on physical education, character education, and spiritual education of the Buddhist youth. Its mission is to train Buddhist youth to be moral, courageous, and righteous, and to help build a positive society in accordance with Buddha's teachings. Since its leaders are volunteer-based, the recruitment and retention is undoubtedly a challenge to firmly keep its vision. The author attempts to find a possible solution for recruiting and retaining its leaders.

At the Vietnamese Buddhist Youth Association, two leadership theories genuinely stand out: servant leadership and authentic leadership. Servant leadership implies that leaders primarily lead by serving others – employees, customers, and the community, whereas authentic leadership demonstrates these five qualities: understanding their purpose, practicing solid values, leading with the heart, establishing close and enduring relationships, and demonstrating self-discipline.

The author recommends that since the VBYA does not have the financial means to compensate and offer rewards, it must focus on training and development in order to recruit and retain its leaders. Additionally, leaders of VBYA must practice and implement the value of leading-by-example (Vietnamese: *Thân Giáo*); it is certainly essential for the success of the organization. The central Buddhist teachings help us transform mindful thought, speech, and actions into our daily lives. Buddha's teachings have reached and transformed numerous people from all walks of life.

Like many other Vietnamese individuals and organizations, VBYA has made many achievements, and although its members also have had a significant number of obstacles, they have managed to adapt, assimilate, and contribute while keeping their distinctive Vietnamese Buddhist ethics and virtues. Vietnamese immigrants have preserved and flourished their unique Vietnamese Buddhist heritage while contributing positively to the cultural and spiritual needs of the Vietnamese and native communities in America.

Introduction

The Vietnamese Buddhist Youth Association (VBYA) was established in Hue City, Vietnam in 1953. Sharing the fate of Vietnamese refugees after the end of the Vietnam War on April 30th, 1975, it came to this country and has flourished ever since. The first Vietnamese Buddhist Youth Association in America, called Cuu Kim Son Buddhist Youth Association, was established in 1976 in San Francisco, CA. Today, there are over 250 chapters of Vietnamese Buddhist Youth Associations all over the United States. VBYA is a non-profit organization that emphasizes not only virtue and moral, ethical and inner values, but also focuses on physical education, character education, and spiritual education of Buddhist youths (GDPT Viet Nam, 2008).

Its vision and mission are to train Buddhist youth to be moral, courageous, and righteous, and to help build a positive society in accordance with Buddha's teachings. According to the GDPT's constitution, its objectives are:

- *To instill in members Buddhist teachings and practice to enable them to live in mindfulness--with peace, joy, and harmony--and empathy with others;*

- *To raise self-esteem and self-support of the spirit among members;*

- *To lead and promote a meaningful and moral social life, healthy in spirit, mind and body; to foster philanthropy among members.*

- *To develop leadership and management skills, creativity, and sense of responsibility in members.*

- *To cultivate communication skills by practicing Right Speech and Deep Listening, and contribute to building strong, happy families and a productive, peaceful society (GDPT Viet Nam, 2008).*

To lead and carry out such ambitions, Talent Management is needed to recruit and retain its manpower. Like any other organization or individual, VBYA wants to be successful. As Carroll (2007) suggests, rules for living our daily lives are relatively straightforward: "Focus on desired results and achieve them as quickly as possible... Amass valuable possessions and avoid unpleasant experiences... Protect yourself unless there is a reason not to." (p. 152).

Unfortunately, it is not that simple for any individual or organization. In fact, many organizations, profit or nonprofit, including the Vietnamese Buddhist Youth Association, are struggling with "desired results" due to the lack of manpower and talent management resources. In other words, these organizations often do not have a defined, successful training, evaluation and retention program. In addition, according to Basarab (2011), there is a lack of reliable strategies and methods to measure what a successful training program and/or evaluation really is.

Purpose

The purpose of this paper is to explore the prevalent leadership theories that are being utilized within the Vietnamese Buddhist Youth Association. Furthermore, it will suggest ways to evaluate personnel and talent management as well as offer advice to recruit and retain its leaders.

Applied Leadership Theories at VBYA

At the Vietnamese Buddhist Youth Association, there are two leadership theories that genuinely stand out: they are

servant leadership and authentic leadership. Servant leadership implies that leaders primarily lead by serving others – employees, customers and the community Greenleaf (1970). Servant leadership has strong links to major religions in the world. In Buddhism, the concept of "serving others is serving the Buddha" is written in the *Kinh Đại Thừa* (Thích, 2011). In Christianity, Arcay (2009) suggests that the root of servant leadership can be traced back to a discussion between Jesus Christ and his disciples as recorded in the Gospel of Luke, chapter 22: verses 24-27. Again, according to Arcay (2009), servant leadership requires the full embodiment of serving God, which means serving with all your heart and soul.

Greenleaf (1970) first coined the term servant leadership in 1970 in his book titled *The Servant As Leader*. It has regained popularity in the last decade due to its strong altruistic and ethical overtones (Northouse, 2004). Greenleaf (1995) described his model as one that encourages "collaboration, trust, foresight, listening, and the ethical use of power and empowerment" (p.1). He argues that servant leadership is serving first with dignity. Customers, employees, and the community as a whole have the highest priority. According to Greenleaf (1995, 2006) and Spears & Frick (1992), servant leadership implies that leaders primarily lead by serving others – employees, customers, and the community. They subjugate their personal needs and desires for the good of the greater community.

In authentic leadership, as George (2008) pointed out, leaders demonstrate these five qualities: 1) understanding their purpose, 2) practicing solid values, 3) leading with heart, 4) establishing close and enduring relationships, and 5) demonstrating self-discipline (p. 92). All of the VBYA leaders volunteer their time, energy and talents. They serve and lead to the best of their abilities. Thus, they are very authentic and sincere in carrying out their tasks. Duchon & Plowman (2005, as cited in DeVost, 2010), point out that spiritual leaders shape work units in a way that allows employees to participate in meaningful work, even in what constitutes "meaningful work" (p. 28) in modern organizational changes. According to Tepper (2003), any individual with a strong inner sense of spirituality will be more likely to find meaning, will be more satisfied with their work, and will contribute significantly more than the non-spiritual one. Additionally, they are more likely to be open-minded, have the ability to experience gratitude for ordinary events, and seek meaning for their spiritual journey as well as have a high intolerance for inequity.

Leadership's Strengths and Weaknesses in VBYA

The leaders in VBYA are all volunteers with a clear mindset to make differences in their lives and in the lives of others. As Alexander Norman writes in the introduction to the book *Beyond Religion-Ethics For a Whole World by His Holiness the XIV Dalai Lama,* "(We need) to come to our own understanding of the importance of inner values, which [the Dalai Lama] believes are the source of both an ethically harmonious world and the individual peace of mind, confidence, and happiness we all seek" (p. xv). In a similar vein, Thich Minh Dat, a spiritual advisor for the Vietnamese Buddhist Community in Northern California, states that anyone of us is an educator because sooner or later, we are all brother/sister, husband/wife, grandfather/grandmother and "If a doctor makes a mistake, he or she can only kill a single person, but if an educator like us makes a mistake, we can kill a whole generation" (Thích, 2011). VBYA's leaders are instilled with this doctrine.

The leaders of VBYA have a strong foundation and follow fundamental principles with defined obligations and responsibilities. The networking between the leaders is similar to a family structure, where they respect and nurture one another. Their minds and hearts are always serving others as well as preserving, protecting, and strengthening the Association's vision and mission. There is a strong relationship among the leaders within their organization and they share similar inner values such as selflessness, sacrifice, and harmoniousness. They also have a high sense of spiritualism and strong moral values. Some of these moral values include compassion, diligence, determination, joy, gratitude, love, integrity, honesty, mindfulness, harmony, perseverance, responsibility, trustworthiness, trust, understanding, and wisdom.

One of the weaknesses of the Association, however, is the lack of a successful recruiting, training, and retention program. Many non-profit organizations, including the Vietnamese Buddhist Youth Association, are struggling with defining the success of their training programs. It is very humbling for the VBYA leaders to carry out their clear vision and mission.

Carroll (2007) contends that humility, simply put, is the absence of arrogance, which means that we engage our work authentically and communicate with others without self-serving agendas (p. 143). Yet, the lack of continuous training and evaluation is a dominant hurdle for VBYA to overcome. Russ-Eft & Preskill, (2009) points out that any training programs or investment in human capital or predictive return must be measurable. To them, evaluation is part of the assessment to improve any organization. Besides not having an adequate assessment process, the financial aspect of the VBYA is also an enormous problem.

Without sufficient funding, it is very difficult to attract and retain talent. According to an article on the *Talent Management* website: "Retaining, Recruiting Top Talent Key Priorities for Employers, Survey Finds" (*Buck Consultants,* May 12, 2011): "Employers are using hiring bonuses to attract talent and retention bonuses to keep them." Furthermore, the two most important components of recruiting and retaining talent are training and development, and compensation and rewards (SHRM Foundation, 2008). VBYA does not have the money to offer these incentives.

Recommendations

Since the VBYA does not have the financial means to compensate its staff and faculty or offer rewards, it must focus on training and development to recruit and retain its leaders. According to the SHRM Foundation (2008) "It takes extensive analysis, a thorough understanding of the many strategies and practices available, and the ability to put retention plans into action and learn from their outcomes. But given the increasing difficulty of keeping valued employees on board in the face of major shifts in the talent landscape, it is well worth the effort" (p. 27). It offers the following advice: "Strengthening employee engagement in your organization can also help you retain talent. Engaged employees are satisfied with their jobs, enjoy their work and the organization, believe that their job is important, take pride in the company, and believe that their employer values their contributions." (SHRM Foundation, 2008, p. 21)

SHRM Foundation (2008) also reveals that "research shows that certain HR practices can be especially powerful in enabling an organization to achieve its retention goals. These practices include (1) recruitment, (2) selection, (3) socialization, (4) training and development, (5) compensation and rewards, (6) supervision, and (7) employee engagement (p.21). Lastly, the SHRM Foundation (2008) concludes:

"To get the most from your retention management plans, you will need to: (1) analyze the nature of turnover in your organization and the extent to which it is a problem (or likely to become one); (2) understand research findings on the drivers of employee turnover and the ways in which workers make turnover decisions; (3) diagnose the most important and manageable drivers of turnover in your company; and, (4) design, implement, and evaluate strategies to improve retention in ways that meet your organization's unique needs" (p. 27).

Additionally, to be consistent with Buddhist philosophy, leaders of VBYA must practice and implement the value of leading-by-example (*Thân Giáo*); it is essential for the success of the organization. According to Bach (2012), "Leading by example is just one invaluable lesson the

Buddha taught us. It is based upon our mindful thought, speech, and actions in our daily life. His teachings have reached and transformed innumerous people from all walks of life. The peaceful development of humanity is in large part due to the enlightened teachings of the Buddha. Today, Buddhism can be a possible solution for the human crises" (p. 5). He suggests that Buddhist youth leaders should establish these guidelines:

Establish a Moral and Ethical Mindset; 2) Understand and Articulate the Principle of Cause and Effect (Law of Karma); 3) Think Globally and Act Locally – making a difference around you first; 4) Demonstrate Mutual Respect and Mutual Benefit; 5) Practice Being Present With Each Other (Presencing) - " Presencing as in the Theory U" - Senge, P. M., Scharmer, C. O., Jaworski, J., & Flowers, B. S. (2005), 6) Engage In The Power of Unity or Collaboration With Other Organizations for Sustainable Change; and 7) Be a (Buddhist) Practitioner, Not Only a Learner (p.6).

As a leader, especially a leader in a Buddhist institution, one must be mindful and have a solid foundation in the Dharma (the teachings of Buddha). As Michael Carroll (2007) suggests in his book, *The Mindful Leader*, the ten talents of a mindful leader are: simplicity, poise, respect, courage, confidence, enthusiasm, patience, awareness, skillfulness, and humility. He continues stating that bringing our full being to work through synchronizing, engaging the whole, inspiring health and well-being in organizations and establishing authenticity, all combine to define a successful leader.

Furthermore, leaders should live a spiritual life and lead by setting positive examples. Another study by Andre L. Delbecq (2008), a professor of Organizational Analysis and Management at J. Thomas and Kathleen L. McCarthy University and Director of the Institute for Spirituality and Organizational Leadership at Santa University's Leavey School

of Business suggests that the managers who are working with him exhibit these positive changes through meditation and spiritual disciplines (p. 495):

- *Improved capacities to listen—less need to dominate*

- *More patience with others—less judgmental and self-asserting*

- *Great adaptability—less desire to control events and others*

- *Great focus—less distraction and anxiety*

- *Greater ability to devote self to service through work— less frustration with burdens and irritants at work*

- *More hopefulness and joyfulness even in times of difficulty—less cynicism and pessimism*

- *Greater overall serenity and trust*

- *More confidence in using personal competencies— deeper knowledge of self-limitations, more trust that things will work out*

- *Persistence and diligence—less withdrawal and self-occupation when under stress*

To Delbecq, nourishing the soul of the leader and inner growth certainly matters. Thus, the spiritual dimension of leadership is particularly crucial and vital for success in any organization.

To emphasize this point, we will examine the work of Vietnamese Zen Master Thich Nhat Hanh. He is a peace activist, a writer, a poet, a scholar, and a Buddhist monk, and is the champion of mindfulness. His work has carried mindfulness practices into mainstream culture. His wisdom and practice of mindfulness have provided guidance and a practical approach, which benefit individuals, families and organizations. Thich Nhat Hanh (1993, 2007) emphasizes: "With mindfulness, we are aware of what is going on in our bodies, our feelings, our minds, and the world, and we avoid doing harm to ourselves and others." He continues: "Mindfulness protects us, our families, and our society, and ensures a safe and happy present and a safe and happy future. Precepts are the most concrete expression of the practice of mindfulness" (p. 2).

Precepts (or *Sila* in Sanskrit and Pali – the ancient language of India) is a "code of conduct that embraces a commitment to harmony and self-restraint with the principle motivation being non-violence, or freedom from causing harm" Bodhi (2005). It can be described in various ways as virtue (Gethin, 1998, p. 170; Harvey, 2007, p. 199), right conduct (Gethin (1998), p. 170), morality (Gombrich, 2002, p. 89; Nyanatiloka, 1988, and Saddhatissa, 1987, pp. 54, 56), moral discipline (Bodhi, 2005, p. 153) and precept.

In the book, *For a Future To Be Possible: Buddhist Ethics For Everyday Life*, Thich Nhat Hanh encourages us to practice the precepts that we have abided to. The five most basic precepts of ancient times (i.e. do not kill, steal, perform sexual misconduct, lie, or use alcohol/intoxicants) still apply for all Buddhists today (Bodhi, 2005; Thich, 1993, 2011). Thich Nhat Hanh (Thich, 1993, 2007, 2011) skillfully and compassionately translated these precepts for our modern time and called them "The Five Mindfulness Trainings". According to him, they "represent the Buddhist vision for a global spirituality and ethics. They are a concrete expression of the Buddha's teachings on the Four Noble Truths and the Noble Eightfold Path, the path of right understanding and true love, leading to healing, transformation, and happiness for ourselves and for the world."

In addition, Thich Nhat Hanh (Thich 1993, 2007, 2011) points out that "to practice the Five Mindfulness Trainings is to cultivate the insight of interbeing, or Right View, which can remove all discrimination, intolerance, anger, fear, and despair." The five ancient precepts were adapted to our modern time under Thich Nhat Hanh's vision as the Five Mindfulness Trainings. They are as follows:

The First Mindfulness Training - Reverence For Life

Aware of the suffering caused by the destruction of life, I am committed to cultivating the insight of interbeing and compassion and learning ways to protect the lives of people, animals, plants, and minerals.

I am determined not to kill, not to let others kill, and not to support any act of killing in the world, in my thinking, or in my way of life. Seeing that harmful actions arise from anger, fear, greed, and intolerance, which in turn come from dualistic and discriminative thinking, I will cultivate openness, non-discrimination, and non-attachment to views in order to transform violence, fanaticism, and dogmatism in myself and in the world.

The Second Mindfulness Training - True Happiness (Generosity)

Aware of the suffering caused by exploitation, social injustice, stealing, and oppression, I am committed to practicing generosity in my thinking, speaking, and acting. I am determined not to steal and not to possess anything that should belong to others; and I will share my time, energy, and material resources with those who are in need. I will practice looking deeply to see that the happiness and suffering of others are not separate from my own happiness and suffering; that true happiness is not possible without understanding and compassion; and that running after wealth, fame, power, and sensual pleasures can bring much suffering and despair. I am aware that happiness depends on my mental attitude and not on external conditions, and that I can live happily in the present moment simply by remembering that I already have more than enough conditions to be happy. I am committed to practicing Right Livelihood so that I can help reduce the suffering of living beings on Earth and reverse the process of global warming.

Phe X. Bach, Ed.D.

The Third Mindfulness Training - True Love (Sexual Responsibility)

Aware of the suffering caused by sexual misconduct, I am committed to cultivating responsibility and learning ways to protect the safety and integrity of individuals, couples, families, and society. Knowing that sexual desire is not love, and that sexual activity motivated by craving always harms myself as well as others, I am determined not to engage in sexual relations without true love and a deep, long-term commitment made known to my family and friends. I will do everything in my power to protect children from sexual abuse and to prevent couples and families from being broken by sexual misconduct. Seeing that body and mind are one, I am committed to learning appropriate ways to take care of my sexual energy and cultivating loving kindness, compassion, joy and inclusiveness – which are the four basic elements of true love – for my greater happiness and the greater happiness of others. Practicing true love, we know that we will continue beautifully into the future.

The Fourth Mindfulness Training - Loving Speech and Deep Listening

Aware of the suffering caused by unmindful speech and the inability to listen to others, I am committed to cultivating loving speech and compassionate listening in order to relieve suffering and to promote reconciliation and peace in myself and among other people, ethnic and religious groups, and nations. Knowing that words can create happiness or suffering, I am committed to speaking truthfully using words that inspire confidence, joy, and hope. When anger is manifesting in me, I am determined not to speak. I will practice mindful breathing and walking in order to recognize and to look deeply into my anger. I know that the roots of anger can be found in my wrong perceptions and lack of understanding of the suffering in myself and in the other person. I will speak and listen in a way that can help myself and the other person to transform suffering and see the way out of difficult situations. I am determined not to spread news that I do not know to be certain and not to utter words that can cause division or discord. I will practice Right Diligence to nourish my capacity for understanding, love, joy, and inclusiveness, and gradually transform anger, violence, and fear that lie deep in my consciousness.

The Fifth Mindfulness Training - Nourishment and Healing (Diet for a mindful society)

Aware of the suffering caused by unmindful consumption, I am committed to cultivating good health, both physical and mental, for myself, my family, and my society by practicing mindful eating, drinking, and consuming. I will practice looking deeply into how I consume the Four Kinds of Nutriments, namely edible foods, sense impressions, volition, and consciousness. I am determined not to gamble, or to use alcohol, drugs, or any other products which contain toxins, such as certain websites, electronic games, TV programs, films, magazines, books, and conversations. I will practice coming back to the present moment to be in touch with the refreshing, healing and nourishing elements in me and around me, not letting regrets and sorrow drag me back into the past nor letting anxieties, fear, or craving pull me out of the present moment. I am determined not to try to cover up loneliness, anxiety, or other suffering by losing myself in consumption. I will contemplate interbeing and consume in a way that preserves peace, joy, and well-being in my body and consciousness, and in the collective body and consciousness of my family, my society and the Earth.

Another seed of strong leadership is leading by example. Venerable Thích Minh Đạt (2011) believes leadership influences by: 1) Teaching by example: teaching through your actions or behavior. One must live a moral and ethical life. Benefit yourself and benefit others, and then influence and contribute positively to our community and society. 2) Teaching by loving speech: seeking understanding and wisdom. 3) Teaching by practicing the Eightfold Path: the first one is of the Right Thought: your thinking must be constructive and always be based on the teachings of the Buddha, with compassion and wisdom.

Conclusion

Thich (2007), a PhD scholar at the University of Florida, concludes that Vietnamese Buddhists are adapting to, interacting with, and assimilating into the American mainstream culture with their Buddhist values. They have made many achievements, and although they also had a significant number of obstacles, they managed to adapt, assimilate, and contribute while keeping their distinctive Vietnamese Buddhist ethics and virtues. He concludes that Vietnamese immigrants have preserved their unique Vietnamese Buddhist heritage, and indeed, their heritage has flourished, while contributing positively to the cultural and spiritual needs of the Vietnamese and native communities in America.

This paper offers the reader an opportunity to look deeply into the leadership at the Vietnamese Buddhist Youth Association and a possible solution for recruiting and retaining its leaders. To fully benefit for the organization, we must know our strengths and weaknesses and seek solutions betterment of the organization.

References

Bach, P. (2012). "Tham luận tại Đại Hội Huynh Trưởng Toàn Quốc Kỳ IX – A 'speech' at 9th National Buddhist Youth Conference in San Jose " Nang Nhon Zen Monastery, San Jose, CA: April 4-8, 2012. Retrieved from "Phe Bach's blog" http://phebach.blogspot.com/p/other-academicresearch-writings.html. On December 08, 2012.

Barnett, R. & Davis, S. (Oct 2008). "Creating greater success in succession planning." Advances in Developing Human Resources,10 (5), 721-739.

Bass, B.M. & Avolio, B.J. (Eds.). (1994). Improving organizational effectiveness through transformational leadership. Thousand Oaks, CA: Sage Publications.

Bennis, W. & Thomas, R. (2002). Crucibles of Leadership. Harvard Business Review.

Bodhi, B. (2005). In the Buddha's Words: An Anthology of Discourses from the Pali Canon. Boston: Wisdom Publications. ISBN 0-86171-491-1.

Bolman, L. G., & Deal, T. E. (2008). Reframing leadership. In J. V. Gallos (Ed.), Business leadership (pp. 35-49). San Francisco, CA: Jossey-Bass.

Buck Consultants (2011, May 12). "Retaining, Recruiting Top Talent Key Priorities for Employers, Survey Finds." See Talent Management website; retrieved   from http://talentmgt.com/articles/view/retaining-recruiting-top-talent-key-prior ities-for-employers-survey-finds/2. On November 14, 2012.

Dalai Lama. (2011). Beyond religion-Ethics for a whole world. Boston: Houghton Mifflin Harcourt.

DeVost, R. (2010). Correlation between the leadership practices of lead ministers and the workplace spirituality of their churches as reported by church members. Andrews University). ProQuest Dissertations and Theses,   Retrieved fromhttp://search.proquest.com/docview/871103857?accountid=105 59

Dierkes, S. (2012). EHRD 604: Development of Human Resources-Week 9 lecture. Retrieved on Nov. 16th, 2012 from https://learn.dcollege.net.

Duchon, D., & Plowman, D. A. (2005). Nurturing the spirit at work: Impact on work unit performance. The Leadership Quarterly, 16, 807-833.

Effron, M., & Ort, M. (2010, May 18). One Page Talent

Management: Eliminating Complexity, Adding Value (1st edition). Harvard Business Review Press.

Employers, Survey Finds." See Talent Management website; retrieved from http://talentmgt.com/articles/view/retaining-recruiting-top-talent-key-prior ities-for-employers-survey-finds/2. On November 14, 2012.

Employers, Survey Finds." See Talent Management website; retrieved from http://talentmgt.com/articles/view/retaining-recruiting-top-talent-key-prior ities-for-employers-survey-finds/2. On November 14, 2012.

Evans, M. G. (1970). "The effects of supervisory behavior on the path-goal relationship". Organizational Behavior and Human Performance, 5, 277–298.

Fullan, M. (2008). The six secrets of change. San Francisco, CA

Jossey-Bass.

GDPT Viet Nam (2008). Nội Quy và Quy Chế Huynh Trưởng; retrieved from "Gia Đình Phật Tử Miền Tịnh Khiết" at http://www.tinhkhiet.org/files/ToChuc/SuMenhDinhHuongGDP TVNHK8.5x11.pdf. On December 08, 2012.

George, B. (2008). Leadership is Authenticity, not style. In Joan Gallos (Editor -2nd edition.), Business Leadership (pp. 87-98). San Francisco: Jossey-Bass.

Gethin, R. (1998). The Foundations of Buddhism. Oxford: Oxford University Press. ISBN 0-19-289223-1.

Gombrich, R. (2002). Theravāda Buddhism: A Social History from Ancient Benares to Modern Colombo. London: Routledge. ISBN 0-415-07585-8.

Greenleaf, R. K. (1970). The servant as leader. Newton Centre, MA: Robert K. Greenleaf Center.

Greif, A. and Laitin, D. (2004). A Theory of Endogenous Institutional Change. American Political Science Review. Vol. 98, No. 4.

Hart, J. (2009). Creating Faculty Activism and Grassroots Leadership. Rethinking Leadership in a Complex, Multicultural, and Global Environment. Kezar, A. (ed.) Stylus.

Hart, R.K., Conklin, T.A., & Allen, S.J. (October, 2008). Individual Leader Development: An Appreciative Inquiry Approach. Advances in Developing Human Resources, 10, 5, 632-650.

Harvey, P. (1990). An Introduction to Buddhism: Teachings, History and Practices. Cambridge: Cambridge University. ISBN 0-521-31333-3.

Heiden, S. (2007). Succession planning: using a bottom-up approach to succession planning. Retrieved from http://www.talentmgt.com/includes/printcontent. php?aid=441, on November 14, 2012.

Hersey, P., Blanchard, K., & John, D. (2001). 8th ed. Management of organizational behavior: utilizing human resources. Upper Saddle River, N.J.: Prentice Hall.

Kubal, D., & Baker, M. (2003, October). "Succession Planning: How Seven Organizations are Creating Future Leaders." Performance Improvement, 42(9), 20-25.

Manderscheid, S.V. & Ardichvili, A. (2008). New leader assimilation: process and outcomes. Leadership & Organization Development Journal, 29, 8, 661-677.

Ñāṇamoli, B. (trans.) (1999). The Path of Purification: Visuddhimagga. Seattle, WA: BPS Pariyatti Editions. ISBN 1-928706-00-2.

Northouse, P. (2004) Leadership: theory and practice (3rd ed.). Thousand Oaks, CA: Sage Publication

Nyanatiloka, Mahathera (1988). Buddhist Dictionary: Manual of Buddhist Terms and Doctrines. Kandy: Buddhist Publication Society. ISBN 955-24-0019-8. Retrieved 2008-02-17 from "BuddhaSasana" at http://www.budsas.org/ebud/bud-dict/dic_idx.htm.

Senge, P. M., Scharmer, C. O., Jaworski, J., & Flowers, B. S. (2005). Presence: An exploration of profound change in people, organizations, and society. Crown Business.

Rothwell, W. J., Jackson, R.D., Knight, S.C., Lindholm, J.E. (2005). Career Planning and Succession Management: Developing Your Organization's Talent-For Today and Tomorrow. Westport, Connecticut, London: Praeger.

Rothwell, W.J. (2010). Effective Succession Planning: Ensuring Leadership Continuity and Building Talent from within (4th edition). New York: American Management Association (AMA).

See EHRD 604: Development of Human Resources Succession Planning Week 8 lecture, 2-26.

Senge, P., et. al. (2005). Presence: Exploring Profound Change in People Organizations, and Society. New York: Currency Doubleday

SHRM Foundation (2008). Retaining Talent. Retrieved 2008-02-17 from "SHRM Foundation – Investing in the future of HR at http://www.shrm.org/about/foundation/research/documents/retai ning%20talent-%20final.pdf

Thích, Đ. (2011, July 11). Leadership Interview with Venerable Thích Minh Đạt/Interviewer: Phe Bach.

Thich, H.N., (1993, 2007). For a future to be possible: Buddhists ethics for everyday life. Berkeley, CA: Parallax Press.

Thich, Q. M. (2007). Vietnamese buddhism in america. (The Florida State University). ProQuest Dissertations and Theses, 465. Retrieved from

http://search.proquest.com/docview/304872348?accountid=10559. (304872348).

CHAPTER 2

MINDFUL LEADERSHIP IN ACTION

Leading by Example - A Buddhist Approach in Leadership and Ethics *

I

n 600 B.C., Prince Siddhartha left his prestigious, glorified and royal life in a quest to search for the answer to ease human suffering. At the end of his six-year-journey and after 49 days of meditation under the Bodhi tree, he reached enlightenment at the age of 35. The teachings of Buddha are based on the foundation of wisdom and compassion through his life experience. Buddhism has been flourishing for 2600 years. His teachings have reached and transformed innumerous people from all walks of life.

Leading by example is just one invaluable lesson the Buddha taught us. "Leading by example" is based upon our mindful thought, speech, and actions in our daily life. The peaceful development of humanity is in large part due to the enlightened teachings of the Buddha. Today, Buddhism can be a possible solution for the human crises. The following seven steps can serve as a solution to many of today's problems.

1 : Establishing a Moral and Ethical Mindset. First, we need to have an idea, or vision, in accordance with the spirit of Buddha's right view. To establish a moral and ethical mindset

One needs thought, speech, and actions that cultivate benefit for oneself and the people around you - not only in the present time, but also in the future. Venerable Thich Minh Dat, a Vietnamese Buddhist monk in Stockton shares his personal mantra: "If a doctor makes a mistake, he or she can only kill a single person, but if an educator like us makes a mistake, we can kill a whole generation." (Thích, 2011).

We ought to acknowledge that we are all educators because sooner or later we are shown to be husband or wife, brother or sister, grandfather or grandmother, etc. We'll have our own children and families. Therefore, we need to educate our children and others the best we can. Likewise, research shows that all good leaders need a moral mindset. But *mindset* alone is not enough; we ought to have a *skillset*. Beside the valuable skills and knowledge, we also need to have a *toolset*. For example, a good teacher is the one who takes his or her students wherever they are and moves them forward in a positive direction. The mindset and skillset are vital, but a toolset, such as school supplies in this case, is also important. Therefore, any educator or leader must have the proper mindset, skillset, and toolset to carry out his or her daily tasks effectively and efficiently.

2.: Understanding and Articulating the Principle of Cause and Effect (Law of Karma): It can be said that everything we have today is a result of our past actions, and that our present actions, words and thoughts determine our future. Understanding this principle helps us to design our own future and destiny. You are in control of your own emotions and well-being. In other words, you are your own creator; your life is depending upon you. What I am today is the result of my actions in the past, and I can foresee my future as it emerges from my actions today. As Buddha says: Orange seeds can only give you oranges and not apples. Therefore, the good or bad deeds or *karma* (Sanskrit: action) that we perform today will dictate our future.

3 : Think Globally and Act Locally – making a difference around you first. There's an old saying: "Be the change that you wish to see in the world." All changes are rooted in one individual first, then the change spreads to the family and finally to the community and society as a whole. For instance: Trash is almost everywhere. If we are aware that trash is an eye-sore or pollution, we'll pick it up and make the environment around us more pleasant. Making changes is just like cleaning up that trash. If we look closely, in our country most of the food we eat travels thousands of miles before it reaches our dinner tables. Going to our farmers markets can make a difference. Buddhists must have a solid foundation of Compassion-Wisdom-Courage, and all of us, including non-Buddhists, must utilize our knowledge, attitudes, and skills.

4 : Mutual Respect and Mutual Benefit. Our tasks and contributions should have as their foundation compassion, wisdom, valor and perseverance to benefit all. We need to acknowledge that the successes of others are also our own successes. The suffering or failure of others is also our suffering and our failure. As leaders, we must see that everything in this world is interconnected and intertwined. Things must co-exist to benefit all communities and societies. This exists because that exists, that exists because this exists or "when this exists, that exists; when this appears, that appears" as written in the Extraordinary Emptiness Sutra. Our modern world is more interdependent now than ever before. The earthquake and tsunami in Japan have affected the world market and people's lives all over the world. The halt in car production in Japan might reduce the workforce in the USA.

The market in China, the earthquake in Turkey, or the Arab Spring in Africa and the Middle East affect our financial, political, and economic well-being. Understanding that everything is interdependent helps us develop empathy, caring and mutual solidarity. Going further, if all of us at all levels in our society put our organizational and community interests and benefits before our own personal interests, then our community and the country will flourish.

5: Being Present with Each Other - (Presencing as in the U Theory). Vietnamese have a saying: "A single swallow does not make a spring." We need to be there for each other and water the positive seeds within each other to make our world a better place to live in.

As Glasl, Lemson and Scharmer said in the U Theory: a) Individuals and teams move through a whole system, integrated planning process involving observation, knowing and visualized decision-making; b) Innovation is integral; c) Policy making (as the elaboration of conscious design principles for the organization) is connected and integrated with the vision of what is to be brought about; d) Relevant to both individual development and practice and organization development and practice, and indeed explicitly connecting these; e) A social technology that contributes to either or both of conflict resolution and social engineering.

Or, as Michael Fullan (2008) in the *The Six Secrets of Change* put it: 1) Love Your Employees; 2) Connect Peers with Purpose; 3) Capacity Building Prevails; 4) Learning Is the Work; 5) Transparency Rules; 6) Systems Learn. We must be there to show our support and our commitment to change. Changes will not come about without our personal commitment. Therefore, we must take a vow to fulfill our responsibilities and obligations both personally and professionally.

6 : The Power of Unity or the Collaboration With Other Organizations for Sustainable Change. Collaborations with other individuals and organizations that have moral foresight and moral core values change the livelihood of others. Any great revolution needs unity. Any change in Buddhism also needs that kind of mutual solidarity. The power of collaboration and networking is needed to create a better change for today and tomorrow.

7 : Be a (Buddhist) Practitioner, Not Only a Learner. In his life, the Buddha's most valuable and practical teachings came from his own lived-experience examples. His leadership style is leading by example in his daily practices and actions. The Buddha's leading by example serves as a guide in our lives. His Sutras, or teachings, are only a means and not a solution. Broadly, the Sutras are what he wanted to teach us, but the ultimate teaching is something we already know, we just need to become aware of it. So please be a worthy practitioner. Thich Dao Quang, a young Buddhist monk at the Tam Bảo Temple in Louisiana, has often reminded us that we all have three lives: our personal or private life, a public life, and an inner, spiritual life. We need to balance them all. In other words, when we take care of our spiritual life, we will have all three lives. So, let us practice transforming our defiled mind into a pure one, and transform our negative and destructive energy into positive and constructive energy.

Nowadays, the development of technology and economics outpaces our spiritual development. Each of us, a Buddha-to-be, whether ordained or layperson, male or female, young or old, whether we are involved in the

Phe X. Bach, Ed.D.

Vietnamese Buddhist Youth Association or not, must learn and practice the art of transforming oneself. Fix that clumsiness or those bad habits and improve your well-being step by step. Furthermore, we need to be optimistic, enthusiastic, and responsible in fulfilling our current roles and functions. A great leader, as Covey (2004) pointed out, also practices four types of intelligences: mental intelligence, physical intelligence, emotional intelligence, and spiritual intelligence. Finally, I use the words of the Most Venerable Thich Minh Dat, who gave me his advice about becoming a transformative leader. He said: 1. Be honest with yourself; 2. Benefit all, not just yourself; 3. Be honest with other people; 4. Be honest and sincere with all the work that you propose.

References:

1 Covey, C. (2004). The 8th Habit: From Effectiveness to Greatness. New York: Free Press

2 Fullan, M. (2008). The Six Secrets of Change: What the best leaders do to help their organizations survive and thrive. (San Francisco: Jossey-Bass). p. 21.

3 Senge, P., et. al. (2005). Presence: Exploring Profound Change in People Organizations, and Society. New York: Currency Doubleday.

4 Senge, P. et al. (2010), The Necessary Revolution: Working together to create a sustainable world, New York: Broadway Books.

5 Thích, Đạt M. (2011). Góp Nhặt Lá Rơi. Stockton, CA. Quang Nghiêm Temple.

6 Thích, Hạnh N. (2007). The Art of Power. New York: HarperOne.

☐ This paper was published for 9th National Buddhist Youth Conference at Nang Nhon Zen Monastery, San Jose, CA. The conference was held from April 4-8th, 2012.

A Leadership Interview with the Most Venerable Thích Minh Đạt:

Examining the Leader-Follower-Situation Dynamic

I interviewed Most Venerable Thích Minh Đạt, Abbot of Quang Nghiêm Buddhist Temple, at his residence in Stockton, CA on July 11th, 2011 at 2:00 PM. I selected the Most Venerable Thích Minh Đạt for this assignment because of his vast experience. He has been a Buddhist spiritual leader for thousands of Vietnamese Buddhists in Northern California and around the United States since 1982. His vision is for the betterment of oneself and the ability to inspire others form the nuances of my leadership style. The purpose of the interview was to inquire about Venerable Thích Minh Đạt's vision and leadership style in relationship to situations and followers. I sent him 17 questions in Vietnamese and English in advance and interviewed him in Vietnamese. Here are the 17 questions in English, which served as the basis for this paper examining the Leader-Follower Situation Dynamic:

1   What is your belief system?

2   Can you name a person who has had a tremendous impact on you as a leader? Maybe someone who has been a mentor to you? Why and how did this person impact your life?

3   What are the most important decisions you make as a leader of your organization?

4   What are your mental models and theory of change?

5   How do you encourage creative thinking within your organization?

6   Where do great ideas come from in your organization?

7   Which is most important to your organization— mission, core values or vision?

8   How do you or other leaders in your organization communicate the "core values"?

9   So, how do you encourage others in your organization to communicate the "core values"?

10 Do you set aside specific times to cast vision to your employees and other leaders?

11 When faced with two equally-qualified candidates, how do you determine whom to hire?

12 What is one characteristic that you believe every leader should possess?

13 What is the biggest challenge that leaders are facing today?

14 What is one mistake you witness leaders making more frequently than others?

15 Can you explain the impact, if any, that social networking and Web 2.0 has made on your organization or you personally?

16 What are a few resources would you recommend to someone looking to gain insight into becoming a better leader?

17 What advice would you give someone going into a leadership position for the first time?

(The Vietnamese version is enclosed in the appendix).

I translated his answers into Vietnamese and emailed back to him to verify for accuracy after the interview. Then, I analyzed his responses using the leader-follower-situation interactional framework (figure 1).

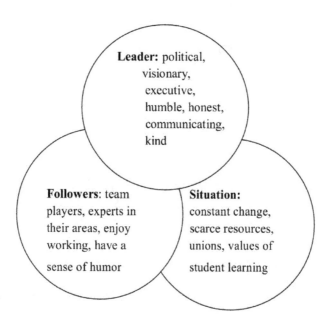

Figure 1. Venerable Thích Minh Đ ạt's Interactional Framework in the Leader-Follower-Situation Dynamic. Adapted from: Hughes, R. Ginnett, R. and Durphy, G. (2006). Leadership: Enhancing the Lessons of Experience. (5th edition). New York, NY: McGraw-Hill/Irwin.

Leader

Venerable Thích Minh Đạt believes that leadership is influenced by: 1) Teaching by example: teaching through your actions or behavior. One must live a moral and ethical life. Benefit yourself and benefit others, and then influence and contribute positively to our community and society. 2)

Teaching by loving speech: seeking understanding and wisdom. 3) Teaching by practicing the Eightfold Path: the first one is of the Right View: your view of actions that are a benefit to you and others at the present moment as well as the future. The Right View leads to the Right Thought, which must be constructive and always be based on the teachings of the Buddha – compassion and wisdom.

He provided very specific examples of his learning and practicing in Buddhism as well as the modeled example set by his master, Thích Thiện Hoa. Venerable Thích Minh Đạt explained his theory of change and his mental model,

"My mental models are built on the foundation of compassion and wisdom. Compassion is vast love to all beings, caring, forgiveness, and tolerance for all species. Wisdom means seeing clearly the path of Buddha's teachings. It also means setting your vision on the greater good for all... All changes generally go through three stages:

"First: One must dedicate and set aside the time to study and experience the teachings of Buddha. Second: One must practice and conduct his teachings daily and properly. Third: One must overcome the difficulties and hardships in order to be successful. Remember that we often encounter obstacles on any path to success or perfection. Often reflect on these issues and resolve them on your own. No one else but you can solve these problems. Patience is the key to success."

Clearly, this fits with Michael Fullan's (2008) "theory that travels." Being an effective leader, also focuses on execution by making sure things get done and are not just talked about (Bossidy, Charan, & Burck, 2008).

Venerable Thích Minh Đạt's most influential mentor is his own teacher, Thích Thiện Hoa, who constantly led by example and gave the advice of, "Do more, talk less." He also embraces his staff and followers, taking time to reflect and make sure any new idea has the consensus of all stakeholders. He practices daily meditation and chanting. This leads to a deeper concentration and, in turn, generates fruitful insights and wisdom. Furthermore, he advises: "You need to have time to think and reflect both on the strengths and shortcomings of yourself and your organization. Seek ideas from others and transform them into something new." Therefore, he purposefully engages all of his stakeholders.

Followers

Venerable Thích Minh Đạt is a Buddhist spiritual advisor and leader in the Stockton area. He is also a spiritual advisor for many Buddhist Vietnamese around the country, especially within Northern California. His vision is far-reaching and commendable. He established Quang Nghiêm Buddhist Temple and has guided the Van Hạnh Buddhist Youth Association since its inception in 1982. Recently, he completed installing the Tháp Phổ Đồng Garden and erecting a statue of Quan Âm, now one of the biggest stone-carved statues in Northern California at 30-feet-tall. In addition, his teaching is practical and applicable.

He has taught us that in order for anyone to make a difference, one must first change and transform oneself. In his leadership role, Venerable Thích Minh Đạt influences change for people around him from young children to our leaders who come from all walks of life. His followers, Vietnamese, Americans, Buddhists, and non-Buddhists alike, are changing the way they live.

One of his students is a retired professor at the University of Pacific in Stockton, CA. Ms. Thu Ngo, treasurer of the Vietnamese Buddhist Association of Sacramento, her husband, Ty Nguyen, and myself are just a few living examples of his students who are transforming their lives through his teachings. His inspiration goes far and beyond the city of Stockton, CA. He is principled and dignified. He is also open-minded to finds ways to solve problems around him. Venerable Thích Minh Đạt's approach is democratic and firm.

Situation

Human needs are dynamic and constantly changing. Therefore, venerable Thích Minh Đạt's decisions are dependent on circumstances, environments, space, and time. As he explains, "One has to be flexible and dynamic at all times; in general it depends on different circumstances, but [the decision] must have a foundation of compassion and wisdom that you set forward."

Venerable Thích Minh Đạt believes that the leader should be sincere about the change process. He also reminds us, "a leader should lead with a greater purpose to benefit all beings; one must put the benefit of the community first." Lastly, he shares, "1 - Be honest with yourself – benefit for all, not just for personal gain; 2 - Be honest with other people; and 3 – Be honest and be sincere with all the work that you propose."

Venerable Thích Minh Đạt and My Own Leadership Development

Venerable Thích Minh Đạt has been teaching and inspiring me for more than a decade. His spiritual and leadership guidance are the foundation for my learning and teaching. Being modest, living a simple life and leading by example are just a few principles that I have learned and practiced. In all, I enjoyed almost a whole day with the most venerable Thích Minh Đạt during the interview process. Lastly, I will always believe in his mantra: "If a doctor makes a mistake, he or she can kill only a single person, but an educator like us makes a mistake, we can kill a whole generation." (Thích, 2011)

Appendix A

Interviewing Leadership Questions in Vietnamese

References

Hughes, R. Ginnett, R. and Durphy, G. (2006). *Leadership: Enhancing the Lessons of Experience*. New York, NY: McGraw-Hill/Irwin.

Thích, Đ. (2011, July 11). *Leadership Interview with Venerable Thích Minh Đạt/Interviewer: Phe Bach.*

CHAPTER 3

MINDFUL LEADERSHIP AND MODERN

TECHNOLOGY

To Be Or Not To Be:

Using Social Media in Teaching

Introduction

I

n 1976, the year I was born, two college dropouts, Steve Wozniak and Steve Jobs, designed and built the first personal computer in a garage at their home. The World Wide Web was first developed by a British software engineer, Tim Berners-Lee, in 1989 (Johnson 2010). Nowadays, we have almost 2.1 billion Internet users as figures show below: (Miniwatts Marketing Group, 2011). Furthermore, the World Wide Web is free, with open access to almost anyone, anywhere. In other words, the Internet is an open context, which is available 24/7/365 (Bonk, 2011).

Applications

Likewise, social media is free and convenient, and millions of students and teachers are using it. I am a "technology immigrant", but the Internet and social media are such hot commodities in education, I debated whether or not I should use social media in my teaching. Before I enrolled in this class at Drexel University, I had very limited experience with social media and open context. But eight weeks into the course, I developed a broader perspective about technology in education. After I finished reading and listening to Bonk (2009), Kurzweil (2005), and *Network models of the diffusion of innovations* by Dr. Thomas Valente (1996), I thought to myself, "I need to be proactive in this educational practice." As Stephen Covey (2004) stated, to "Be proactive" is the first of seven habits of an effective leader. The positive energy that I garnered from the executive meetings during the lectures and discussions has motivated me to find new ways to utilize our technology.

Potential Impact

What surprised me the most is the work of Ray Kurzweil in *The Singularity Is Near* (2005). The future is so distant, yet it is so near. We are making material progress and achieving the heights of knowledge. It is very likely due to the ongoing acceleration of technological developments that our standard of living will evolve substantially, since evolutionary growth proceeds exponentially (Kurzweil, 2005). It is very difficult for me to think about and imagine the future technological world. Yet the insight and wisdom of Kurzweil has enlightened me. As he concludes: "Our ability to create models--virtual realities--in our brains, combined with our modest-looking thumbs, has been sufficient to usher in another form of evolution: technology" (p. 487).

Conclusion

Due to my better understanding of technology's role in our society today and in the future, I set up a Twitter account for the first time and I reactivated my Facebook account. I am starting to use them more often. For the coming school year, I plan to actively use social media as an educational tool. Not only I am going to use it to communicate with my students, but I will also use it as a formative assessment. Formative assessment is a reflective process that helps educators to adjust their teaching strategies as well as promote student attainment and help students refine their own learning. Using social media can be a great tool to support our students to learn more effectively and efficiently.

References

Bonk, C. (2009). The World is Open: How Web Technology is

Revolutionizing Education. San Francisco: Jossey-Bass.

Covey, S. (2004). The 8th Habit: From Effectiveness to

Greatness. New York: Free Press.

Kurzweil, R. (2005). The Singularity Is Near. New York:

Penguin Group.

Miniwatts Marketing Group (2011), World Internet Users and Population Stats. Retrieved from http://www.internetworldstats.com/stats.htm

Valente, T. W. (1996). Network models of the diffusion of innovations. *Computational & Mathematical Organization Theory, 2*(2), 163-164.

Why iPads Should Be Used in Public Schools: The Foundation and Vision for the 21st Century

Technology in Public School

Introduction

Imagine the first day of school at Mira Loma High School, which was built in 1960. A young teenage boy with an overloaded backpack walks down an overcrowded hall and bumps into another student. Books and supplies fly everywhere and the mayhem begins. Imagine in the same scenario, a teenage girl holding her iPad2 walks down the hall with her headphones in her ears, listening to a Lady Gaga music video. All eyes would look at her and everyone would say, "That is awesome." Education can be cool when iPads are used as digital textbooks, a personal library, an entertainment hub, and a personal student assistant.

On a similar note, here is a more personal story. During the summer, I decided to take a job where I could give something back to the community, helping others while earning a few dollars for a summer vacation. That job was teaching refugees, mostly Iraqis and Nepalese, who immigrated to the United States of America less than a year ago. As a refugee myself, I am sympathetic and understanding of the struggles and needs of refugees. I thought that my experience learning English could be a helpful tool for teaching them as well. But as it turned out, our society is extremely technologically advanced compared to 20 years ago when I arrived in the United States. When I studied English, I used post-it notes and wrote on them: "This is a desk, thing that you can touch; that is a girl, thing you can't touch, etc." That was how I learned English. Nowadays, we are using iPads to teach refugees, which is truly fascinating. iPads can be an amazing and exciting tool in our education system. People learn in multiple ways – some by reading, some by hearing, and some by seeing. The iPad as a tool enhances the teacher's method of communicating more effectively, and increases the students' range of learning.

The Background and Evolution of iPads

The history of iPads is a continuation of Apple's development of tablet computers. Their first tablet computer, was developed but not introduced to the market. Later, Apple released different models of PDAs, but discontinued its last version in 1998. In 2007, Apple returned to the mobile-computing market and has had great success with iPhones and almost three years later, Apple announced the arrival of the first iPad in April 2010. According to the Apple's website (2011), within the first 80 days three million iPads were sold.

iPads Applications

As Nutting, Wooldridge, & Mark (2010) pointed out, "Unless you've been living under a rock, you're well aware that the new darling in Apple's product line is the iPad, a thin, touch screen table that aims to revolutionize mobile computing and portable media consumption." It is convenient, can be used as a GPS, an iPod, a digital library, and many other applications.

In our refugee classrooms, my co-worker Armando and I explored and used many different apps. The students got hooked on learning with the iPads. From read-aloud texts to coloring books, these resources are basic and vital resources for newcomers. We used the following apps: Wikipanion; Grammar Up, Translate This, Speak it, Newsy, iQuestion, ABC Writing, Doodle Buddy, iSentence, vBookz, TimeReading, Vocabulary, Sight Words, and BrainPOP. Some of the digital tools we used are: YouTube, video, games center, iBooks, and AudioBooks. Other students explored exciting iPad apps, such as iAnnotate PDF, ReelDirector, Writing Pad, Pages, and QuickOffice. Our curriculum changed to accommodate iPad activities. Students were curious and enthusiastically engaged in different activities.

Additionally, Nutting et al. (2010) stated that "many presentations created on Macs or Windows computers work perfectly when transferred to the iPad... [The iPad] has education apps and videos range in topics from farming to astro-dynamics and range from content for kindergartners to graduate students." In other words, they argued "iTunes University is the perfect destination for anyone who desires to further their knowledge."

The Future of Pads in Education

More than ever, life is more convenient, increasingly beautiful and full of magic thanks to these technological innovations. Possibilities seem endless, including people getting closer over distances, using FaceTime. iPads could be used as digital textbooks in the very near future. Alan Hess (2001) asked such basic questions as "Can the iPad be used as an educational tool? Apple believes that it can. Is this practical? Can teachers and students use the iPad for educational purposes, or is it just a big toy? Well, I believe wholeheartedly that the iPad can be an invaluable tool for high school and college education, and it can be used to enhance education at all levels" (p. 269). Overall, with the development of software and apps, the future of iPads in education is very near and realistic.

Advantages and Disadvantages of iPads in Education

Vineet Madan (2011), Vice President of McGraw-Hill

Higher Education eLabs, offered six reasons why iPads and other tablets should be implemented in our classrooms. First, tablets are the best way to show textbooks. Second, classrooms are ready for tablets. Third, tablets fit students' lifestyles. Fourth, tablets have the software to be competitive. Fifth, tablets integrate with education IT trends. Lastly, tablets are becoming more readily available.

His argument is based on the iPad pilot program at Reed College that tested the Kindle DX e-readers. That device was considered a failure for

Phe X. Bach, Ed.D.

use in classrooms. The report found that, in contrast, "the iPad's responsive and smooth scrolling touch screen made it ideal for reading content in the classroom. Navigation among passages was quick and easy. The highlighting and annotation of text was also easy, with many students choosing to highlight text on the iPad over traditional pen and paper."

There are other good arguments for using iPads. According to Mark Crump (2010) "the iPad is going to succeed in education marvelously for students and teachers." He gave many advantages and a few cons. Here are the advantages over other e-tablets: "1) Good battery life and lightweight, 2) "Bag of Holding" for class materials, 3) Easy to do work in the library, 4) No laptop stigma, and 5) Single-tasking may let one focus better" while one of the main arguments against using the iPad is: "No full-size keyboard (speculation)." Sande et al. (2010) argued that you can use "the iPad as a travel computer or a remote to your computer desktop via iTeleport apps." Furthermore, this new technology also has the ability to allow users to adjust text size and screen brightness, which aids those with vision challenges.

Based on personal experience, iPads can be a distraction to students and lead them off-task. For example, whenever I was not watching them closely, students tended to use their iPads for entertainment purposes. Believe it or not, sometimes students are more interested in watching videos on YouTube than learning. Therefore, lesson plans must be structured and classroom management well-executed in order for iPads to work effectively. One of the techniques I learned from a colleague is

94

"Tech-off and Tech-on Time," (Tech-off is when every student put the keyboards upside down and not use their computers and Tech-on is when they can use them), which offers some great opportunities for direct instruction and collaborations among students.

Bonk (2009) explains, "collaborative tools bring ideas, talents, resources, networks, and products together for sharing and innovation" (p. 524.) He continues that use of technology such as iPads "for global knowledge sharing includes massive online libraries of searchable and reusable data, vast numbers of online courses, and online portals of digital information. And there are innovative and far less expensive tools for collaboration than what was available a decade or two ago. The convergence of these factors allows for greater human participation, interaction, and knowledge sharing" (p. 249-252.)

From five years back, education has been facing a significant financial challenge. In every school and district in California budgets have been reduced substantially each year. Financial resources are limited and funding is low for all schools. Many programs are being eliminated. Music, languages, and art are just a few casualties of this difficult financial time. Students have limited options to choose their elective classes. Unfortunately, schools and districts do not have the money to buy iPads for each student or classroom to implement this clever new technology in our classroom yet. However, each district, as required by the federal government, must still have money to buy textbooks. Buying iPads as a form of alternative textbooks is a golden opportunity. Districts can also collaborate with other organizations to locate funding for a greater sustainable change.

References

Apple Sells Three Million iPads in 80 Days". (2010, June 22).

Retrieved from http://www.apple.com/pr/library/2010/06/22ipad.html.

Bonk, C. (2009). The World is Open: How Web Technology is

Revolutionizing Education. San Francisco: Jossey-Bass

Guy, Retta (2009). The Evolution of Mobile Teaching and

Learning. Santa Rosa, CA: Informing Science Press.

Hess, A., (2011). IPad 2 Fully Loaded. Indianapolis: Wiley

Publishing, Inc.

Madan, V. (2011). 6 Reasons Tablets Are Ready for the Classroom, Mashable.

Nutting, J., Wooldridge, D., & Mark, D. (2010). Beginning IPad Development for IPhone Developers: Mastering the IPad SDK. New York: APress.

Sande, S., Sadun, E., Grothaus, M., (2010). Taking Your IPad to the Max. Google eBook.

6 Reasons Tablets Are Ready for the Classroom (n.d.) Mashable. Retrieved from http://www.ipadinschools.com/284/why-the-ipad-should-be-used-in-classrooms/

Global Kids – Youth Leaders for 21st Century: A Case Study of an Innovative Approach in New York Public Schools

Background/History of the Technology Used in the Project

When I was a child, I believed that children were the future leaders of our society. Discovering Global Kids, Inc. reassured me that this viewpoint is still valid. Global Kids, Inc. was founded by award-winning educator Carole Artigiani in 1989, although it didn't incorporate until 1991. She was its executive director from its incorporation until August of 2010.

According to its website http://globalkids.org/media.php?pageID=36, the primary mission of Global Kids is to develop youth leaders for the global stage through dynamic global education and leadership development programs. "Global Kids inspires underserved youth to achieve academic excellence, self-actualization and global competency, and empowers them to take action on critical issues facing their communities and our world." One of its successful programs is the implementation of the Digital Media for 21st Century Skills via Online Leadership Program

(OLP), which "integrates international and public policy issues into digital media programs to encourage digital literacy and technical competency, foster global awareness, promote civic participation and

develop   21st   Century   skills."
(http://globalkids.org/media.php?pageID=36)

Applications of the Technology

Global Kids takes advantage of open web content to introduce best practices over the school year. In its OLP programs, high school students learn how to communicate and express their perspectives and opinions regarding domestic and global issues. Students effectively use online games, virtual worlds, and social media to promote their ideas. The students invent Games for Change and conduct public programs via the virtual world of Teen Second Life. Furthermore, they document and share with others, including their peers, educators, and researchers all over the world. "At the same time, digital media is used as a tool for alternative assessments practices, using digital portfolios and game-like badges to document and motivate interest-driven learning," the website added.

(http://www.parentguidenews.com/Articles/YoungLeadersinthe Making)

Potential Impacts of the Technology

The idea that we need to "share the wealth" is vital for a sustainable change in our world. This is analogous to our planetary food resources: we don't have a problem with food shortage; we do have a problem with food distribution. In education, the openness and willingness to share professional curriculum development with others via "open context" is commendable. As a case in point, the goals of Global Kids are achievable and encouraging. Those who have used this program have a higher than ninety percent high school graduation rate, despite the challenges youth face in underserved communities like inner city urban neighborhoods. The video on its website also mentioned that close to ninety percent of participants go on to attend college and many earn scholarships. Furthermore, some Global Kids alumni become civic leaders, champions of social justice and successful professionals in our society. Some continue to advocate for social action and global engagement.

Pros and Cons of the Technology and Approach

Global Kids has year-round programs online, in schools, and at their headquarters, which means it is available to help more students. It serves thousands of middle school and high school students in inner city neighborhoods. It is a modeled program for many others around the world. It also provides capacity building services and professional development services for youth leaders, educators, and institutions for New York City's Department of Education and Department of Youth and Community Development (DYCD), New York Public Libraries, and other institutions serving youth. The topics that Global Kids provides include global citizenship, youth development, conflict resolution, facilitation, digital/games-based learning, bias awareness, and more.

Phe X. Bach, Ed.D.

Implications for Leadership Decision-making

The essence of Wagner's (2008) argument is that today, in the 21st Century, our students and teens must have these seven survival skills: 1) Critical Thinking and Problem-Solving; 2) Collaboration across Networks and Leading by Influence; 3) Agility and Adaptability; 4) Initiative and Entrepreneurialism; 5) Effective Oral and Written Communication; 6) Accessing and Analyzing Information; and 7) Curiosity and Imagination.

Carole Artigiani realized the importance of these sills and transformed her thinking into action. Today, as Artigiani put it: "Global Kids has worked with more than 120,000 students and educators in New York City and beyond, receiving national recognition for exemplary practices in international education, digital media programming, experiential learning, and youth development. Our work is enhanced by our strong partnerships."

References

"2010 GK - Developing youth leaders for the global stage." (2011, July 22). Retrieved from http://globalkids.org/media.php?pageID=36

Friedman, T. (2007). The world is flat: the globalized world in the twenty-first century. New York: Penguin.

Mindful Leadership

Wagner, T. (2008). The global achievement gap: why even our best schools don't teach the new survival skills our children need – and what we can do about it. New York: Perseus Books Group.

Planned Change: Leadership and Evaluating Change

Introduction

Buddha said: "Everything is impermanent." In other words, change is happening in every moment. Change, whether planned or unplanned, occurs at every level: individuals, families, organizations and/or communities. According to Cummings & Worley (2009), we change "to solve problems, to learn from experience, to reframe shared perceptions, to adapt to external environmental changes, to improve performance, and to influence future changes" (p. 22). Since change is inevitable, a better question is: How do we respond to external change with the best internal change? We change for the betterment of ourselves, our families, organizations and everything around us. The foundation for change must come from within; a happy individual contributes to the well-being and happiness of a family, and ultimately contributes to a better society. We change ourselves first, and then interact with changes in our world.

Organizations use "planned change" to improve performance, to cut operational costs, or both. Individuals plan changes in lifestyles, habits, and values in order to transform themselves in a positive direction. At all levels, from individuals to organizations, we are geared toward improving efficiency and effectiveness. However, all change, whether planned or unplanned, comes with costs and benefits. Keep in mind that the outcome of a planned change may be different than we had expected due to many situational forces (Cummings & Worley, 2005). In this paper, I discuss planned change and how change is essential and good, since it makes an organization and company improve in response, as well as making life more interesting, more challenging and more beautiful.

Planned Change

Planned change is one of the hot topics in organizational development (Cummings & Worley, 2005). Planned change is geared toward improving the effectiveness and efficiency in any operation; his topic has attracted the attention of many scholars and analysts, including, but not limited to, Kotter (1995), Benne & Chin (1985), and Cummings & Worley (2005).

According to Cummings & Worley (2005), planned change "involves a series of activities for effective organization development" (p.39). In any organization, whenever things are not working as expected, "leaders in the organization recognize the need for a major change and establish strategies to accomplish its objectives" (Cummings & Worley, 2005, p. 27). Planned initiatives are undertaken in order to transform, to innovate, and to prosper in a competitive and ever-changing environment. In order to properly execute planned change, leaders must reflect and evaluate during the implementation stage to determine the effectiveness of the planned change. The resulting feedback empowers the "key players" to refine plans and strategies, ensuring that the current change plan or future change initiatives are successful (Cummings & Worley, 2005).

Phe X. Bach, Ed.D.

Challenges and Solutions

Challenges are numerous, yet they're perfect opportunities for leaders to make a great impact on the organization. Leaders of organizations have the obligation and responsibility to decide which plan should be implemented for the challenges they face. Challenges can be structural, financial, technical, or involve the work culture. Planned change in an organization is a vital process that modifies the organizational system, improves the work atmosphere, and tackles ongoing organizational issues.

The solution that results from planned change comes in many shapes and forms. The "planned change may be implemented in a variety of ways, depending on the client's needs and goals, the change agent's skills and values, and the organization's context" (Cummings & Worley, 2009, p. 29). Leaders must find creative ways to solve problems. First, leaders must have a clear vision and mission that all stakeholders buy into. Stakeholders must clearly see that not only would benefit they individually, but also the entire organization would benefit from the collective effort to bring about changes, allowing members to become more productive, enhance their job performance and improve their work culture. Second, guidelines for change can be found in the Fullan's Six Secrets of Change (2008). The six secrets are:

1 **Love Your Employees** – Enable employees to learn continuously and find meaning in their work, build internal relationships, while training staff in new approaches.

2 **Connect Peers with Purpose** – Provide good direction for staff to pursue implementation through purposeful

3 Peer interaction and learning. Get staff involved in necessary change.

4 **Capacity Building Prevails** – Build capacity in the organization by investing in knowledge and skills of individuals, ensuring wise use of resources, and motivating all stakeholders to put in energy for results.

5 **Learning Is The Work** – Leverage the consistency-innovation continuum. One must accomplish goals through relentless consistency while simultaneously demonstrating innovation

6 **Transparency** – Share results with all stakeholders.

7 **Systems Learn** – All individuals in the system live by the five previous tenets while shaping the organization.

Through effective communication, group dynamics, and action research, we can implement any "planned change" while learning from it. Continuously improving quality, practices and values is a great building mechanism for any organization.

General Model of Planned Change

There are three main models of Planned Change. Here, I focus on the Action Research model by Kurt Lewin (1946), since he is widely recognized as the founding father of Organizational Development. Lewin believes that change can be an effective and efficient path leading to permanent social change via action. He reasons that if stakeholders are active in the decision-making process, they are more likely to adopt new ways. He named this concept "rational social management" (p. 155). Lewin's process of change has three steps: 1) "Unfreezing": Faced with a dilemma or disconfirmation, the individual or group becomes aware of a need to change; 2) "Changing": The situation is diagnosed and new models of behavior are explored and tested; and 3) "Refreezing": Application of new behavior is evaluated, and if reinforcing, adopted. Lewin's change process can be summarized in the figure below.

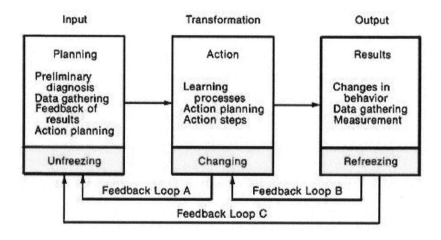

Figure 1: Systems Model of Action-Research Process, Prokapenya (2005).

This figure provides a summary of the steps and processes involved in planned change via rational social management. The first stage of planning, called Unfreezing, involves the input for understanding the forthcoming planned change. Management needs to initiate change, working together with all stakeholders to perform a preliminary diagnosis, gather data, review results, and jointly plan the next actions. Then, in the action or transformation phase, "Changing," stakeholders learn the process to plan and execute behavioral changes. Finally, stakeholders obtain results, reflect and alter the previous planning, if necessary, to bring the activities just learned into better alignment with the organization's goals and objectives, "Refreezing".

Conclusion

Planned change is an effort to increase an organization's performance, relevance and viability. While planned change can be and time-consuming, as Seeger, Ulmer, Novak and Sellnow (2005) point out, it allows organizations to explore ways to respond to the opportunities in any crisis to change or transform. It is an ongoing, systematic process that requires lots of attention, resources, energy and willpower to bring about true transformations. As Ralph Emerson once said:

"What lies behind us and what lies before us are tiny matters compared to what lies within us." So, first, let us ask what lies within each of us individually and collectively in our organization. Then we can begin our changes from within.

Phe X. Bach, Ed.D.

References

Benne, K. & Chin, R. (1985). "Strategies of change." In Bennis, W., Benne, K. & Chin, R. (editors), *The Planning of Change.* New York: International Thompson Publishing.

Cummings, T. & Worley, C. (2009) *Organizational development and change*, 9th Edition. Mason, OH: South Western.

Cummings, T.G., & Worley, C.G. (2005). *Organization development and change.* Thomson-South-Western.

Fullan, M. (2008). *The six secrets of change: What the best leaders do to help their organizations survive and thrive.* San Francisco: Jossey-Bass.

Kotter, J. (1995). "Leading change: why transformation efforts fail." *Harvard Business Review,* 73(March), p.59-67.

Lewin, K. (1946). Action research and minority problems. *Journal of social issues, 2*(4), 34-46.

Lippitt, G. (1969). *Organizational renewal.* Englewood Cliffs, NJ: Prentice-Hall.

Ravid, R. (2011). *Practical statistics for education (4th Ed.).*

Rowman & Littlefield, Inc., Lanham, MD.

Seeger, M. W., Ulmer, R. R., Novak, J. M., & Sellnow, T. (2005). Post-crisis discourse and organizational change, failure and renewal. *Journal of Organizational Change Management, 18*(1), 78-95. Retrieved from http://search.proquest.com/docview/197603273?accountid= 10559

Prokopenya, Viktor, Systems Model of Action-Research Process. 15 May 2008. (From Wikipedia, the free encyclopedia. Organization development. Retrieved from

http://en.wikipedia.org/wiki/Organization_development

ORGANIZATIONAL DEVELOPMENT INTERVENTIONS

Interventions: To be effective and efficient

Introduction

Here I elaborate on the meaning of "intervention" and focus on how to design an effective intervention for an organization's positive development. In our rapidly-changing technological culture, every organization must respond appropriately to change in order to remain profitable in a competitive setting. In other words, an organization must set a solid vision with a clear mission statement, and then follow a series of planned changes and interventions to continue to achieve shared goals. Then, this paper explores four major types of interventions and the conditions for them to be effective.

Interventions and Organizational Development

In recent years, interventions in organizational development have been studied extensively (McNamara, 2009; Cummings & Worley, 2005). According to Cummings & Worley (2005), "The intervention refers to a set of sequenced planned actions or events intended to assist an organization increase its effectiveness. Interventions purposely disrupt the status quo; they are deliberate attempts to change an organization or subunit toward a different and more effective state" (p. 143). Or in other words, the intention of interventions is to improve organizational performance and to increase the effectiveness of both the employer and the employees.

In order to both understand and design effective organizational development interventions, we need to look into the organization's issues. Before discussing the four types of interventions, the leadership at any organization must also recognize the four types of issues. According to Cummings & Worley (2005), there are: 1) strategic issues, which determine what products or services to provide; 2) technological and structural issues, which determine how to divide the work into different departments and how to coordinate them; 3) human resource issues, which attract and retain competent employees; and 4) human process issues, which determine the social process such as communication and decision making (Cummings & Worley, 2005). These four issues must be understood by the top leadership of the organization, and all employees at different levels must support the interventions. Understanding these issues helps leaders to design effective interventions.

According to many researchers, there are various types of interventions for organizational development depending on the particular situation or environment (Lewicki & Sheppard, 1985). Cummings & Worley (2005) and McNamara (2009) pointed out that there are four different kinds of interventions: 1) human process interventions, 2) techno-structural interventions, 3) human resource management interventions, and 4) strategic interventions. I will briefly discuss these interventions and how they are related to organizational development.

1. Human Process Interventions:

According to Cummings & Worley (2005) human process interventions are related to individual competencies, interpersonal relationships, and group dynamics. They include but are not limited to coaching, training and development, process consultation, third-party intervention, and team building. These strategies help to build a stronger relationship and interpersonal communication. Likewise, McNamara (2009) mentions that any training and development must include "human process intervention" (p.156).

2. Techno-structural Interventions:

As the name would indicate, this type of intervention focuses on an organization's technology and structure. It is meant to increase productivity and human fulfillment (Cummings & Worley 2005). This type of intervention also may include design, downsizing, and reengineering (Cummings & Worley, 2005 p. 151). We often hear in the news about jobs being shifted overseas and many companies laying off their employees - a polite way to say they are "downsizing". Both of these measures are a direct result of this type of intervention.

3. Human Resource Management Interventions:

These interventions include the practices of career planning, reward systems, goal setting, and performance appraisal. In other words, the intervention is designed to improve individual and group performance and employees' working relationships in the organization (Cummings & Worley, 2005; Cummings, 2008). They also point out three methods of change to assist organization members: 1) Career planning and development, where the organization provides help to employees so they may choose career paths and attain career objectives; 2) Managing workforce diversity, where human resource practices are made more responsive to a variety of individual needs; and 3) Employee stress and wellness, where employees are provided with help for stress management and other work-related issues of well-being. All of these interventions seek to change specific features or parts of the organization (Cummings & Worley, 2005).

4. Strategic Interventions:

These interventions are relatively new to organizational development (Cummings & Worley, 2005). They are meant to shape the competitive and collaborative strategies and culture in the following ways: a) Integrate strategic change, to gap the transition period between old and new, b) Mergers and acquisitions, to help form a new entity, c) Alliances, to pursue a set of private and common goals through sharing, and d) Networks, to help develop relationships with three or more organizations to perform tasks and solve problems that an individual organization can't solve alone (Cummings & Worley, 2005).

The success of any intervention is dependent on leadership and the buy-in of all stakeholders. Kotter (2011) points out that it takes the kind of leader who can create a vision, bring people together, and communicate in such a way to steer people through change. Furthermore, the ability to implement most organizational development interventions is highly dependent on the skills and knowledge of the change agent (Cummings & Worley, 2005, page 144). Also, intervention requires the imagination and creativity of the leadership.

Conclusion

Organizational development interventions are essential and dynamic. It takes strong leadership in an organization with a commitment to change and all stakeholders must support it. According to Fullan (2008), the process must be transparent. He points out, "By transparency, I mean openness about results. I also mean openness about what practices are most strongly connected to successful outcomes" (p. 99). Transparency is essential to success (Fullan, 2008) and strong communication must prevail (Salem, 2008).

George Bernard Shaw's words are fitting here: "Imagination is the beginning of creation. You imagine what you desire. You will what you imagine and last you create what you will."

References

Cummings, T. & Worley, C. (2005). *Organization development and change.* Mason, OH: South Western.

Cummings, T.G. (2008). *Handbook of organization development* (editor). Thousand Oaks, CA: Sage Publications.

Fullan, M. (2008). *The six secrets of change: What the best leaders do to help their organizations survive and thrive.* Jossey-Bass - John Wiley and Sons, Imprint.

Kotter, J. (2001).   *Kotter international: because change is essential.* Retrieved from http://www.kotterinternational.com/

Lewicki, R. & Sheppard, B. (January 1985). *"Choosing How to Intervene: Factors affecting the use of process and outcome control in third-party dispute resolution."* Journal of Occupational Behavior, 6, p.49-64.

McNamara, C. (2009). *"Organizational Change and Development: Managing change and change management."*

Online@http://managementhelp.org/organizationalchange/index.htm#anchor72711; retrieved August 2, 2012.

Salem, P. (2008). *"The seven communication reasons organizations do not change."* Corporate Communications: An International Journal 13 (3), p. 333-348.

Senge, P.M. (2006). *The Fifth Discipline: The Art & Practice of the Learning Organization* (Revised). New York: Currency- Doubleday.

Leadership in Change

Introduction

What is the role of leadership in change initiatives? First, we need to know what defines leadership. Corneilus & Associates (2011) suggested that "there are five critical qualities that a leader must have." To them, a leader must be a visionary; a leader must be a person of integrity and honesty and have strong values; a leader must know how to properly motivate others; a leader must be able to lead change; and finally, a leader must be able to lead a culture of change.

Thus, leading a change initiative is crucial for any organization's success. Arguably, it is one of the most difficult tasks that any leader may face. Still, leadership must be authentic. Authentic leaders, as George (2008) pointed out, demonstrate these five qualities: 1) understanding their purpose, 2) practicing solid values, 3) leading with heart, 4) establishing close and enduring relationships, and 5) demonstrating self-discipline (p. 92).

Leadership and Change

According to Cummings & Worley (2005), "Organization transformation implies radical changes in how members perceive, think, and behave at work. These changes go far beyond making the existing organization better or fine-tuning the status quo" (p. 480). These transformational changes require creativity, innovation, learning and reflection of the leadership and the organization to improve its outcome.

Transformation changes can start with cultural change. William Ouchi in his *Theory Z* points out that the best management tends to promote stable employment, high productivity, and high employee morale and satisfaction (Ouchi, 1981). Additionally, Cummings & Worley (2005) mentioned that the organization's culture change "include[s] the artifacts, norms, values, and basic assumptions that are more or less shared by organization members. The meaning attached to these elements helps members make sense out of everyday life in the organization" (p. 483).

In short, these transformations occur at all levels from individual change to culture change. In an organization, changes may begin with any employee, up to the top executive. As Cummings & Worley (2005) put it, "changing corporate culture can be extremely difficult and requires clear strategic vision, top-management commitment, symbolic leadership, supporting organization changes, selection and socialization of newcomers and termination of deviants, and sensitivity to legal and ethical issues" (p. 509).

Change Theories

I will explore two different outstanding and well-accepted views in leading change in our modern world: the leader-centric (top-down) approach and the participative (bottom-up) approach. I will also explore some other leadership theories such as Transformational leadership,

Principle-Centered Leadership, and Aspirational and Visionary Leadership.

According to Conger (2005), the leader-centric, or top down approach, can make a direct and effective change. Kotter (2009) adds that top-down leadership is in the unique position of affecting change and he outlines eight steps or models as follows: "[a]cting with urgency, developing the guiding coalition, developing a change vision, communicating the vision buy-in, empowering broad-based action, generating short-term wins, don't let up, and make change stick." On the other hand, the bottom-up (participative) approach involves empowering the employees' participation in the decision-making process of the organization. This practice enables the "bottom" to voice their opinions and gives their input for transformation within an organization.

Transformational Leadership

Transformational leadership is one of the most accepted leadership theories of modern times. Bass and Avolio (1994) believe that leaders and followers help each other to achieve and advance. They claim that a transformational leader is charismatic and has a vision, which inspires followers to work harder in order to achieve their shared goals. Transformational leaders provide followers with a strong sense of purpose. Furthermore, as Bass and Steidlmeier (1998) note, "The literature on transformational leadership is linked to the long-standing literature on virtue and moral characters, as exemplified by Socratic and Confucian typologies." However, it was first introduced by Burns (1978) who bases his theory on a foundation of a social-historical perspective with an incorporation of moral development and mutual interdependence of human interaction.

According to Burns (1978), transformational leadership is a process wherein "leaders and followers raise one another to higher levels of morality and motivation." He celebrates the fact that followers are assumed to transcend self-interest for the good of the group, consider long-term objectives, and develop an awareness of what is important. Whereas, according to Bennis (2005), "Effective leaders perform the three functions: align, create and empower." He goes on to argue that leaders transform organizations by aligning human and other resources, creating an organizational culture that fosters the free expression of ideas, and empowering others to contribute to the organization.

Moreover, Bennis distinguishes the difference between leader and manager most clearly. He states, "Leaders are people who do the right thing; managers are people who do things right." Lastly, Yukl (2006) urges that transformational leadership is the business of engaging, motivating and inspiring other people to achieve a shared vision or purpose. Besides that, it needs to move far and beyond self-interest, and consider what is best for the organization or for the greater good.

Aspirational and Visionary Leadership

Aspirational and Visionary Leadership - Burns (1978); Kouzes & Posner (1995, 2002); Peters, Waterman (1990); Richards & Engle (1986). According to Kouzes and Posner, leaders ignite subordinates' passions and serve as a compass by which to guide followers. They define leadership as "the art of mobilizing others to want to struggle for shared aspirations."

The emphasis lies in the follower's desire to contribute and the leader's ability to motivate others to action. Leaders respond to customers, create a vision, energize employees, and thrive in fast-paced "chaotic" environments. Leadership is about articulating visions, embodying core values, and creating an environment within which things can be accomplished. Additionally, Kouzes and Posner (1999) add that the aspirational and spiritual component of leadership is the "practice of encouraging the heart". In their book, titled *Encouraging the Heart*, Kouzes and Posner wanted to add "our voices to the discussion of soul and spirit in the workplace.

Leaders create relationships, and one of those relationships is between individuals and their work. Ultimately, we all work for a purpose, and that purpose has to be served if we are to feel encouraged" (p. xv). They went on and identified seven essential components to this caring relationship: (a) setting clear standards, (b) expecting the best, (c) paying attention, (d) personalizing recognition, (e) telling the story, (f) celebrating together, and (g) setting the example.

Recommendations

I believe that both Conger's top-down approach and Bennis's bottom-up (participative) approach have both advantages and disadvantages in leading change. As Dr. Moffitt put it, both have "merit", yet leading change must be holistic. Interpersonal relationships must be built and the professional gap must be bridged among members of any organization in order to establish long-lasting changes.

Likewise, according to Cummings & Worley (2005) leading changes must start with "self-designing organizations that have the built-in capacity to transform themselves to achieve high performance in today's competitive and changing environment" (p. 493).

Conclusion

Leading change is essential and difficult. Yet, it is vital for the development of any organization with a solid mission statement and a clear vision. It must start from within each individual. Herold & et al. (2008) found that "Transformational leadership and individuals' commitment to change were significantly positively related." Also, according to Fullan (2008), any leading change must be transparent. Transparency is essential to success (p. 100) and strong communication must prevail (Salem, 2008). Lastly, Cummings & Worley (2005) point out that it "helps the organization move beyond solving existing problems and gain the capability to improve continuously" (p. 479).

References

Bennis, W. (2005), Reinventing Leadership: Strategies to Empower the Organization. Reading, MA: Addison-Wesley.

Conger, J.A. (1994). Spirit at work: Discovering the spirituality in leadership. San Francisco: Jossey-Bass

Cornelius & Associates. (2011). The Qualities of Leadership: Motivating Others. www.corneliusassoc.com

Cummings, T. & Worley, C. (2005). Organization development and change. Mason, OH: South Western.

Cummings, T.G. (2008). Handbook of organization development (editor). Thousand Oaks, CA: Sage Publications.

Moffitt, B. (2012b). EHRD 601: Week seven video lecture Good Work Now. Retrieved from Drexel University Blackboard Learn.

Fullan, M. (2008). The six secrets of change: What the best leaders do to help their organizations survive and thrive. Jossey-Bass - John Wiley and Sons, Imprint.

Herold, D. M., Fedor, D. B., Caldwell, S., & Liu, Y. The effects of transformational and change leadership on employees' commitment to change: a multilevel study. Journal of Applied Psychology. 2008, Vol. 93, No. 2, 346-357.

Kotter, J. (2001). Kotter international: because change is essential. Retrieved from http://www.kotterinternational.com/

Ouchi, William G. (1981). Theory Z: How American Business Can Meet the Japanese Challenge. Addison-Wesley.

Salem, P. (2008). "The seven communication reasons organizations do not change." Corporate Communications: An International Journal 13 (3), p. 333-348.

Phe X. Bach, Ed.D.

Senge, P.M. (2006). The Fifth Discipline: The Art & Practice of the Learning Organization (Revised). New York: Currency-Doubleday.

CHAPTER 4

MINDFUL LEADERSHIP AND CASE STUDIES

Learning From The Mistakes of Others – When Leading Without Compassion...

L

eadership without moral values can be devastating. The actions of an incompetent leader, particularly Captain Francesco Schettino of the cruise ship *Costa Concordia*, is an example. On January 13, 2012, the pleasure cruise ship *Costa Concordia* embarked on a seven-day journey through the Mediterranean Sea. It left the port just north of Rome heading for Morocco. This goliath boat, which was owned by Genoa-based Costa Cruises in 2006, was believed to be the largest cruise ship under the Italian flag at that time.

There were about 4,200 people on board the ship. The crew was performing their daily tasks, and passengers were enjoying their Mediterranean voyage. The journey started uneventfully, as a typical day at sea. Nearly three hours into the journey, however, the captain decided to deviate from the ship's authorized route to showcase the boat to the locals of the Island of Giglio who enjoy looking at the cruise ships from shore. Suddenly, at 9:30 PM the cruise ship hit a rock in shallow water off the Island of Giglio. Chaos and lack of communication ensued, leading to 17 deaths and leaving 15 missing persons. As Bennis and Nauus (1985) once said: "Managers do the things right, and leaders do the right thing" (Bolman & Deal, 2008, p. 36). The captain, Francesco Schettino, did neither.

The lack of leadership and poor decision-making of the captain allegedly led to unprecedented numbers of deaths. The captain's actions included deviation from a set route, delaying passenger evacuations, abandoning ship after the disaster while the passengers were still aboard, and refusal to return to the ship to lead rescue efforts when ordered to do so by local port officials. The lack of direction, leadership, and communication made the disastrous situation even worse. After the collision, the crew failed to communicate with the passengers to announce what had occurred. While in chaos, the captain was among the first individuals to abandon the ship before the passengers were rescued, and refused to return to the ship to aid in rescue efforts.

First and foremost, a leader is also a manager. He or she must carry out immediate tasks as well as envision a long-term solution. Kotter (2008) points out that "Management develops the capacity to achieve its plan by organizing and staffing—creating an organizational structure and set of jobs for accomplishing plan requirements, staffing jobs with qualified individuals, communicating the plan to those people, delegating responsibility for carrying out the plan, and devising systems to monitor implementation" (Kotter, 2008, p. 6). During the accident, the captain did not do his job as a manager. His lack of responsibility and obligation were evident during the crisis.

The massive casualties could have been avoided even after the ship ran aground. Lack of leadership by the captain exacerbated the problem. The captain had none of the five dimensions of authentic leadership as defined by George:

1   Understanding the purpose

2   Practicing solid values

3   Leading with heart

4   Establishing close and enduring relationships

5 Demonstrating self-discipline (George, 2008, p. 92)

The captain forgot the purpose of the voyage, and deviated from the set route that he was supposed to follow. Once the boat hit the rock, he did no leading whatsoever; instead, he ordered himself a good meal and abandoned the ship before the passengers had a chance to get to safety. The captain was neither practicing solid values nor leading with heart. Nor did he demonstrate self-discipline. As Heifetz and Linsky (2008) pointed out, "Self-knowledge and self-discipline form the foundation for understanding one's leadership in adaptive change environments" (pages 163 – 206). The captain apparently lacked both self-knowledge and self-discipline.

Heifetz and Linsky presented the metaphor of the "dance floor" and the "balcony" to help leaders understand the types of challenges and problems faced on a daily and long-term basis. Schettino's lack of knowledge, absence of hard-working ethics, and shortage of enthusiasm further escalated the disaster.

Captain Francesco Schettino ought to have led by example and taken charge, but he failed miserably. He wasn't able to sustain himself as a leader, with no apparent ability to see the dangers that were coming. He forgot about the "dance floor" (Heifetz & Linsky, 2002) that he was supposed to choreograph. He also did not go up to "the balcony" to observe, reflect and lead. The lack of reflection (or looking down from the balcony) hindered his ability to see the crisis at hand.

From the captain's deck, he could see the floating "iceberg" (Senge et al., 2010) and the huge problems that he was facing. "Leaders develop the habits of mind and competencies to lead complex organizations shaped by global forces." (Senge et al., 2010) Clearly, the captain was not able to develop that kind of habit. While on the balcony, the entire picture should be seen more completely and, he should have understood that help was available to him. In other words, Heifetz & Linsky suggest, "Getting to the balcony, finding partners, adjusting the thermostat, pacing the work, making your interventions unambiguous and timely, bringing attention back to the issue, and showing the relevant communities a different future than the one they imagine are all methods of dealing with the disequilibrium that you generate" (Heifetz & Linsky, 2002 p. 160). The captain did not seem to evaluate the dangerous situation at all. Russ-Eft & Preskill (2009) tell us that the leader must decide what ought to be the case and provide information to all stakeholders, which in this case were the people on the boat and the first responders.

If, once up on the balcony level, Captain Francesco Schettino had applied the three-legged stool: seeing systems, collaborating across boundaries, and creating desired futures (Senge, Smith, Kruschwitz, Laur & Schley, 2010), the result would have been more satisfactory. On another note, the captain violated his ethic of caring; he didn't "consider multiple voices in the decision-making process." (Shapiro & Stepkocich, 2005, p.18). As leaders, we must set a clear mission, have core values and have the capacity to transform ourselves. The third keystone in our program is just that: leaders develop the abilities to sustain their own leadership growth.

To put it clearly, the ideal captain should be authentic; his constructive actions must take place with a great deal of moral courage. As George (2008) explains: "The values of the authentic leader are shaped by personal beliefs, developed through study, introspection, and consultation with others—and a lifetime of experience" (George, 2008, p. 94). It would have behooved the captain to have practiced some of the foundations of leadership such as Kouzes and Posner's Five practices of exemplary leadership: 1) model the way, 2) inspire a shared vision, 3) challenge the process, 4) enable others to act, and 5) encourage the heart (Kouzes & Posner, 2008, p. 26). Should he have had solid values, he could have led this disaster effectively and efficiently. As Kouzes & Posner (2008) once again point out: "To effectively model the behavior they expect of others, leaders must first be clear about their guiding principles" (p. 27).

In summary, the crisis of the cruise ship *Costa Concordia* in Italy, caused entirely by Captain Francesco Schettino, is an unforgettable lesson for any leader. First, leaders must guide by practicing solid values (George, 2008) and modeling the way (Kouzes & Posner, 2008). By learning from the lived experience (phenomenology) of the incompetent leader-- Captain Francesco Schettino, we will more greatly value the keystones of our program: 1. *Leaders develop the abilities to sustain their own leadership growth* and 2. *Leaders develop the habits of mind and competencies to lead complex organizations shaped by global forces.*

Finally, let's remember as Gallos (2008) pointed out, "Failure gives you a second chance to learn" (p.479).

Case 2: *Please note that Sacramento Chronicle is a fiction name for any big newspaper company in the USA.*

In a declining economy such as the one we are experiencing, businesses face challenges, yet have opportunities to flourish. The leadership at Sacramento Chronicle is no exception. Declining newspaper subscriptions, wavering employee morale, and a documented inability to "connect" with younger, more tech-savvy clientele have given the leadership team a clear picture of the impending threats to their own sustainability. Now, they ought to look at the leadership structure and different strategies in order to overcome the obstacles and challenges they are facing. This is very much related to the first keystone in our program: "possess the abilities to create and support communities that are the bases for sustainable change".

Heifetz & Linsky (2002) reminded us that leadership "challenges us intellectually, emotionally, spiritually and physically" (p. 163). I. e., as the new leaders at Sacramento Chronicle, ought to "motivate people in a variety of ways" including, but not limited to, a) articulate the organization's vision in a manner that stresses values, b) regularly involve people in deciding how to achieve the organization's vision, c) support employees' efforts to realize the vision by providing coaching, feedback, and role modeling, and 4) recognize and reward success (Kotter, 2008, p. 12).

As the consultant team from 4-Gone Conclusion, we also need to understand that "A sustainable future will entail collective creating of every imaginable sort" (Senge, Smith, Kruschwitz, Laur & Schley, 2010 p. 50). We must work collaboratively to generate a suitable strategy for sustainability of The Sacramento Chronicle. Adaptive change involves collaborating across boundaries in the "three-legged stool" (Senge et al., 2010).

We must implement Fullan's six secrets of change: "1. Love your employees. 2. Connect with purpose, 3. Capacity building prevails, 4. Learning is the work. 5. Transparency rules. And 6. Systems learn." It must be noted that "'Love your employees' is meant to apply to large-scale reform. The goal is to change whole organizations, whole systems" (Fullan, 2008 p. 10) and "connect peers with purpose is understood as synergistic" (Fullan, 2008 p.10). Yet it is healthy to keep in mind that the company must walk a balanced path into the future.

As Senge et al (2010) commented: "Leaders want to learn how to ride the wave of sustainability innovation into the future while still maintaining healthy and viable business in the present" p. 119). In other words, the company is encouraged to apply the last keystones of the EdD program at: "Exemplify the curiosity, inquiry skills, and scholarly competencies needed to investigate an idea and transform it into meaningful action."

That meaningful action is the beginning of a strategic and collaborative transformation.

The future of newspapers has changed and so has the readership. As Competency Question One pointed out: "While the declining economy was manifested in sharp declines in newspaper subscriptions, more and more customers are opting to visit the Chronicle's basic website for news content." According to Bonk (2011) the Internet is an open, which is available 24/7/365 and learner/reader participation in the Open Information Communities is continuous.

The competency question continued, "Social media and other forms of rapid information sharing threaten the very relevance of the newspaper, which served to be the bread and butter of this organization for more than a century. The imminent change strikes fear in the aging employee base that was very accustomed to the steady roles associated with creating and delivering the daily newspaper." The Sacramento Chronicle should keep in mind that "technology by itself will not empower learners. Innovative pedagogy is required" (Bonk, 2009, p. 33). Thus the company must transform itself to adapt into the new environment.

In other words, it must accept the fact that "before you begin something new, you have to end what used to be." (Bridges, pg. 23). To attract a younger readership, the content must be attractive and rich in beautiful, lively graphics. The change "will entail collective creating of every imaginable sort" (Senge et al., p. 50). Social media is also a new part of integration of the Chronicle.

The interaction between the readers and the newspaper will be part of the sustainable change. Being green is also a new magnet for younger readers. "Momentum for change starts to build when people see the cost-effectiveness of going further than compliance in the state, which is just trying to meet minimum legal requirements in areas such as air emission, toxic waste, and wastewater" (Senge et al., p. 115). It is a means to boost a new kind of advertising revenue as well. This distinction is very important because the new leadership team must learn to "utilize the full range of emerging technologies to reach across generations, communicate effectively, and engage others in meaningful change" as tattooed in our EdD program's 4th keystone.

Moreover, the leadership team at Sacramento Chronicle should implement the "Twelve categories of systems that leaders use to affect behavior" (O'Toole, 2008). They are:

1 Vision strategy: Extent to which corporate strategy is reflected in goals and behaviors at all levels

2 Goal-setting and planning: Extent to which challenging goals are used to drive performance

3 Capital allocation: extent to which capital allocation decisions are objective and systematic

4 Group measurement: Extent to which actual performance is measured against established goals

5 Risk management: Extent to which the company measures and mitigates risk

6 Recruiting: Extent to which the company taps the best talent available

7 Professional development: Extent to which employees are challenged and developed

8 Performance appraisal: extent to which individual appraisals are used to improve performance

9 Compensation: extent to which financial incentives are used to drive desired behaviors

10 Organizational structure: Extent to which decision-making authority is delegated to lower levels

11 Communications: Extent to which management communicates the big picture

12 Knowledge transfer: Extent to which necessary information is gathered, organized and disseminated. (p. 54)

Lastly, people are often resistant to change. These dramatic changes will impact the organization and its stakeholders. However, all changes require strong visions and visions require an act of faith. As Nanus (2008)

echoes: "A vision portrays a fictitious world that cannot be observed or verified in advance that, in fact, may never become reality. It is a world whose very existence requires an act of faith" (p. 313). The new leadership team at Sacramento Chronicle must acknowledge that they are "acting in the world and not on the world" (Scharmer, 2007), (Senge, P., et. al. 2005). As Scharmer (2007) concluded, "When that shift happens, people begin to operate from a future space of possibility that they feel wants to emerge. Being able to facilitate that shift is the essence of leadership today."

In conclusion, knowing that the leadership challenges at the Sacramento Chronicle are numerous provide an opportunity for leadership growth and organizational change. Yet with innovative strategies and a new kind of leadership the company can turn around. As Gallos (2008) put it the "Success in leadership, success in business, and success in life has been, is now, and will continue to be a function of how well people work and play together. Success in leading will be wholly dependent upon the capacity to build and sustain those human relationships that enable people to get extraordinary things done on a regular basis." (p.33)

References:

Bonk, C.   (2009). The World is Open: How Web Technology is Revolutionizing Education. San Francisco: Jossey-Bass

Fullan, M. (2008). The six secrets of change. San Francisco, CA: Jossey-Bass.

Heifetz, R. A., & Linsky, M. (2002). Leadership on the line; staying alive through the dangers of leading. Boston, MA: Harvard Business Review Press.

Kotter, J. P. (2008). What leaders really do. In J. V. Gallos (Ed.), Business leadership (pp. 16-25). San Francisco, Ca: Jossey-Bass.

Kouzes, J. M., & Posner, B. Z. (2008). The five practices of exemplary leadership. In J. V. Gallos (Ed.), Business leadership (pp. 26-34). San Francisco, Ca: Jossey-Bass.

Nanus, B. (2008). Finding the right vision. In J. V. Gallos (Ed.), Business leadership (pp. 311-232). San Francisco, Ca: Jossey-Bass

O'Toole, J. (2008). When leadership is an organizational trait. In J. V. Gallos (Ed.), Business leadership (pp. 50-60). San Francisco, Ca: Jossey-Bass.

Russ-Eft, D., and Preskill, H. (2009). Evaluation in Organizations: A Systematic Approach to Enhancing Learning, Performance and Change, Second Edition. New York, NY: Perseus Books.

Senge, P., et. al. (2005). Presence: Exploring Profound Change in People Organizations, and Society. New York: Currency Doubleday.

Senge, P., Smith, B., Kruschwitz, N., Laur, J., & Schley, S. (2010). The necessary revolution. New York, NY: Broadway Books.

AN IDEAL LEADERSHIP

Leadership with a passion is ideal and invaluable. This is a unique opportunity for Dr. Ida Ruiz, a newly-hired dean, to make her legacy. Yet, she entered the Woods Community College with "mental models of that community college education always has been and would be (set)". This mindset can be an obstacle if she is not willing to make a mental adjustment. With the pre-determined mindset of Dr. Ruiz, that could be difficult. However, her situation would be better off if she follows these three recommendations.

First and foremost, like Dr. Bureau, the director of Sacramento EdD program, once said: "My mental model is a WIP". It is a Work-In-Progress. With a dynamic educational environment and a diverse culture and society, anything that is set in stone or pre-determined will not be successful. The complexities of coping or initiating change in everyday situations (dance floor) vs. long-term (balcony) views must be adopted. Dr. Ruiz is a new leader in a very different time.

As Heifetz & Linsky (2002) pointed out: "Adaptive change stimulates resistance because it challenges people's habits, beliefs, and values" (p. 30). First, Dr. Ruiz needs to get on the "dance floor" and implement everything in her skill-set and tool-set that she brings to the college. Secondly, she ought to use the balcony approach to look for patterns of behavior of all stakeholders. This is a great chance for her to reflect and grow in the first phase of her appointment. The movement between the "dance floor" and the "balcony" is vital for her survival. When Dr. Ruiz takes her dances to the floor and integrates the big picture or ideas developed on the balcony, she is learning to adjust for a better future.

Second, Dr. Ruiz needs to be open-minded. She can evaluate her current programs, staff and the needs for school. Russ-Eft & Preskill (2009) offered that "the leader must decide what ought to be the case and provide information to all stakeholders". Once she gets solid feedback, she can decide if she needs to re-evaluate the data and seek potential alternative solutions. It is vital to point out that our students have modern of needs and skill sets for the 21st Century. According to Wagner (2008), our students and teens must have these seven survival skills: 1) Critical thinking and Problem-solving; 2) Collaboration Across Networks and Leading by Influence; 3) Agility and Adaptability; 4) Initiative and Entrepreneurialism; 5) Effective Oral and Written Communication; 6) Accessing and Analyzing Information; and 7) Curiosity and Imagination.

It is crucial for us to understand our intertwined world. Conventional wisdom has it that the world is getting smaller because of technology. According to Bonk (2011), the Internet is an open context, which is available 24/7/365 and learner/reader participation in the Open Information Communities." In his book *The World is Open: How Web Technology is Revolutionizing Education,* Bonk (2009) pointed out the essence of the technology to enhance learning.

1   Web Searching in the World of e-Books;

2 **E**-Learning and Blended Learning;

3 Availability of Open Source and Free Software;

4 Leveraged Resources and OpenCourseWare;

5 Learning Object Repositories and Portals;

6 Learner Participation in Open Information Communities;

7 Electronic Collaboration;

8 Alternate Reality Learning;

9 Real-Time Mobility and Portability;

10 Networks of Personalized Learning

It is essential to utilize emerging technologies for teaching and learning. The funding can be a challenge, but "where there is a will, there is a way" and Ruiz needs to prioritize the budget accordingly. However, given that we are almost two decades into the 21st Century, technology is the lungs of education that we can't live without. Technology is also one of the five keystones in our EdD program. We are living in a modern society, and must utilize "the full range of emerging technologies to reach across generations, communicate effectively, and engage others in meaningful change."

Third, all changes must start within and they can be learned. That is of the six secrets of change. According to Fullan (2008), the Six Secrets of Change are: "1. Love your employee; 2. Connect with purpose; 3.

Capacity building prevails; 4. Learning is the work; 5. Transparency rules; 6. Systems learn. He also emphasized that systems learn in two ways: "They focus on developing many leaders working in concert, instead of relying on key individuals and, second, they are led by people who approach complexity with a combination of humility and faith that effectiveness can be maximized under the circumstances" (p. 109). As long as the stakeholders feel valued in building a collective capacity for a shared vision, Dr. Ruiz will be successful in her endeavors.

In conclusion, a leader must be dynamic and flexible to adapt to their new environment. A leader must have the skills and insights to achieve their goals and objectives. We are a technologically advanced nation; we need competitive advantages in education in order to prepare our young for the global market; therefore, we must implement technology to produce high quality learning experiences and to bring our education system to the next level. We must be innovative.

CHAPTER 5

MINDFUL LEADERSHIP AND PRACTICES

A POTENTIAL SOLUTION

FOR MODERN LEADERS

N

owadays, it is very common to have factions and tensions within any company or organization. A great leader must have a clear vision and solid mission to unify all stakeholders to create a better company or organization. Heifetz & Linsky, (2002) once said: "The challenge of leadership, when trying to generate adaptive change, is to work with differences, passions, and conflicts in a way that diminishes their destructive potential and constructively harnesses their energy" (p. 102). Everybody in any company or organization would like to contribute positively to his or her workplace. They want their company/organization to flourish, to improve, and to be successful. Max A. Millian must "possess the abilities to create and support communities that are the bases for sustainable change." I would propose these three principles to salvage the future of Structural Engineering.

1 : Establish a "mindful" movement.

First we need to have an idea, a vision that benefits everyone inside and outside of any company, organization or institution. Keep in mind that what contributes to a mindful movement is thought, speech, and action that work together to cultivate benefit for yourself, your organization and the people around you - not only in the present time, but also in the future. This is the Art of Mindfulness. One must learn that they must not fret or be worried about things that have not yet come, like the man who has the cow must not be worried over losing the cow. (Thich, 2010). It is through the power of awareness that we recognize where the organization really is and make adjustments to move forward. Mindfulness can be a strange concept to the Westerner, but it is actually very simple. However, it is nearly impossible to master without practice. It is the art of completely utilizing our senses, along with one hundred percent of our focus to do any task in our lives; in this case using the collective energy to move any company forward or organization in a positive direction. It is another step in the chain to attain true power. It will lead to more awareness and happy employees as well as a productive and successful company.

This is what Senge and Scharmer called "presencing". The essence of presencing is that two selves — our current self and our best future one — meet at the bottom of a U and begin to listen and resonate with each other. Once a group crosses, nothing remains the same. Individual members and the group as a whole begin to operate with a heightened level of energy and sense of future possibility. They then begin to function as an intentional vehicle for an emerging future, and that is what the company needs.

We are "acting in the world and not on the world". This is the great concept that Max Millian will have to perform and implement with his colleagues, team leaders/managers and employees. With this mindful approach, both the leaders at the company and the employees should adopt the changing culture and embrace the transformation of the company.

2 : Balancing the Ethic of Critique and the Ethic of Care of the company.

The company needs to be mindful of where it is and where it is headed. If the company has a divided and tense staff, it is vital to critique and reflect for a constructive purpose. It is disheartening when there is a lack of concern for ethics in such a professional setting. What the company needs are different kinds of ethics: "1. Ethic of Justice; 2. Ethic of Diversity - race, ethnicity, religion, social class, gender, disability, sexual orientation; 3. Ethic of critique, and 4. Ethic of care." (Schapiro & Stepkocich, 2009). They must be understood, shared and implemented as a whole staff. The two ethics of critique and care are a must to change the culture of the company. As Schapiro & Stepkocich (2009) pointed out, the Ethic of Critique is based on the critical theory, which as its heart, recognizes an analysis of social class and its inequalities (p. 14). These inequalities can be between groups or departments within the organization. It is their inequitable contribution that causes the company's decline. Furthermore, organization must emphasize the Ethic of Care. The Ethic of Care is not only essential in education, but also in any setting such as a professional company like Structure Engineering. According to Burns: "Ethics reflect modes of more formal and transactional conduct—integrity, promise-keeping, trustworthiness, reciprocity, accountability— supremely expressed in the golden rule" (Burns, 2008, p. 306). It is the drive for everyone to excel and to contribute positively.

3 : Establishing Unity and Collaborative Culture for Sustainable Change.

Collaboration between different stakeholders within the company is crucial. The product development, engineering, and marketing divisions must communicate and collaborate with each other. Any great revolution needs unity. Changes in the company will need mutual solidarity. Additionally, there needs to be collaboration with other departments within and outside of the organization.

Senge et al. (2010) indicated that "Collaborating is ultimately about relations, and relationships do not thrive based on a rational calculus of costs and benefits but rather because of genuine caring and mutual vulnerability" (p. 233). Collaboration is the foundation for the company to grow not only financially, but also to grow in ease and less stressful of a working environment. They continued: "We have found that building this collaborative capacity rests on three capabilities: convening, listening and nurturing shared commitment" Senge et al. (2010) p. 233. Everyone needs to contribute mutual respect and understanding to improve Structure Engineering. More importantly, Max needs to lead through his own actions; he must not only "talk the talk", but also "walk the walk". Perhaps, as Bolman & Deal (2008) encouraged, we all need the "characteristic of symbolic leadership" to carry out changes. They are:

2   Symbolic leaders lead by example

3   Symbolic leaders use symbols to capture attention

4   Symbolic leaders lead from experience

5   Symbolic leaders communicate a vision

6   Symbolic leaders tell stories

7   Symbolic leaders respect and use history (p. 46-48)

In short, the power of collaboration and networking are needed to create a better change for today and tomorrow. The leader must be the one to show action passionately on the "dance floor" and reflectively on the "balcony" as well as leading by his or her own example.

To transform the culture of Structural Engineering at the salvageable stage, Max A. Millian must be insightful, strong, and innovative in carrying out these three recommendations. 1. Establishing a "mindful" movement for everyone; 2. Balancing the Ethic of Critique and the Ethic of Care for everyone; and 3. Establishing unity and collaborative culture for sustainable change for the company. With his strong and ethical mindset and his devotion, Max will develop, "the habits of mind and competencies to lead complex organizations shaped by global forces" (Drexel EdD's 2nd keystones) not only for himself, but for everyone at Structural Engineering.

PERSONAL REFLECTION ON MINDFULNESS

I would like to share some of my personal practices that I find very helpful in mindful leadership and I am inviting you to practice as well. Here is its original version:

Mindfulness is the energy of self-observation and awareness of what is going on around you and within you. Mindfulness brings you back to the present moment. The present moment is the only thing we truly have because, *yesterday is history and tomorrow is mystery. Today is the gift*—the here and now. Mindfulness enables us to focus, clear our mind, and enhance our loving-kindness. We all, including our students, know on some level that the future is dictated by what we are thinking, speaking, and acting at this moment. Everything we do has a consequence; and consequences can be positive or negative. Thus, if the students would like to have an A in the future, they must work hard at this very moment. At the beginning of the semester remind them that everyone is getting an A, but how to retain that A is another story. It is like love or being in a marriage: falling in love or getting married is an easy stage, but how you remain in love or stay married is an art and science in itself.

A Mindfulness-based approach enables us to do just that--remain in love, stay married, or keep the A. This is a life-skills that today's students need. I often ask my students these questions, and I reflect often upon them as well. The questions are: "Are we part of the problem or part of the solution? and "What direction are we heading?" In terms of anything in our life: academics, finances, spiritual growth, our relationship to others-- including our siblings, friends, romantic partner, parents, and everyone else. If that "A" or that door, the gateway, to a better future is our aim, our goal, then are we heading in the right direction? Are we really moving toward that, with everything we do, say or think?

Let's say, as an example to our students: Imagine you have $5 for your allowance each day. In the morning you spend $3 on your Starbucks coffee and in the afternoon you spend another $3 on your Jamba Juice. You have $5 and spend $6—in what direction are you going financially? You are going in a negative direction. You're going to get a negative balance. In fact, you are going backwards just like Michael Jackson's moonwalk. Thus, you need to be mindful, recognize your own actions, stop going backwards and move in a positive direction toward your set goals. A philosopher once pointed out that it

doesn't matter how slow or how fast we are going, as long as we are going forward in the right direction. To get to the right direction, I am practicing some of the practices based upon the teaching of Zen Master Thich Nhat Hanh of Plum Village in French. Here are a few practices:

BEGINNING ANEW

To begin anew is to look deeply and honestly at ourselves, our past actions, speech and thoughts and to create a fresh beginning within ourselves and in our relationships with others. At the practice center we practice Beginning Anew as a community every two weeks and individually as often as we like.

We practice Beginning Anew to clear our mind and keep our practice fresh. When a difficulty arises in our relationships with fellow practitioners and one of us feels resentment or hurt, we know it is time to Begin Anew. The following is a description of the four-part process of Beginning Anew as used in a formal setting. One person speaks at a time and is not interrupted during his or her turn. The other practitioners practice deep listening and following their breath.

Flower watering – This is a chance to share our appreciation for the other person. We may mention specific instances that the other person said or did something that we had admired.

This is an opportunity to shine light on the other's strengths and contributions to the Sangha and to encourage the growth of his or her positive qualities.

Sharing regrets – We may mention any unskillfulness in our actions, speech or thoughts that we have not yet had an opportunity to apologize for.

Expressing a pain – We may share how we felt hurt by an interaction with another practitioner, due to his or her actions, speech or thoughts. (To express a pain we should first water the other person's flower by sharing two positive qualities that we have truly observed in him or her. Expressing a pain is often performed one on one with another practitioner rather than in the group setting. You may ask for a third party that you both trust and respect to be present, if desired.)

Sharing a long-term difficulty & asking for support- At times we each have difficulties and pain arise from our past that surface in the present. When we share an issue that we are dealing with we can let the people around us understand us better and offer the support that we really need.

The practice of Beginning Anew helps us develop our kind speech and compassionate listening. Begin Anew is a practice of recognition and appreciation of the positive elements within our Sangha. For instance, we may notice that our roommate is generous in sharing her insights, and another friend is caring towards plants.

Recognizing others' positive traits allows us to see our own good qualities as well.

Along with these good traits, we each have areas of weakness, such as talking out of our anger or being caught in our misperceptions. When we practice "flower watering" we support the development of good qualities in each other and at the same time we help to weaken the difficulties in the other person. As in a garden, when we "water the flowers" of loving kindness and compassion in each other, we also take energy away from the weeds of anger, jealousy and misperception.

We can practice Beginning Anew everyday by expressing our appreciation for our fellow practitioners and apologizing right away when we do or say something that hurts them. We can politely let others know when we have been hurt as well. The health and happiness of the whole community depends on the harmony, peace, and joy that exists between every member in the Sangha.

Source:

http://plumvillage.org/mindfulness-practice/beginning-anew/

SOLITUDE

Although in our daily lives, we are constantly with the Sangha, we are also in solitude. Solitude is not about being alone high up in the mountains, or in a hut deep in the forest, it is not about hiding ourselves away from civilization. Real solitude comes from a stable heart that does not get carried away by the crowd nor by our sorrows about the past, our worries about the future, and our excitement about the present. We do not lose ourselves; we do not lose our mindfulness. Taking refuge in our mindful breathing, coming back to the present moment is to take refuge in the beautiful, serene island within each of us.

We participate together with the Sangha for sitting meditation, walking, meals, working, but always we are within our own island as well. We can enjoy being together with our brothers and sisters, but we are not caught and lost within emotions and perceptions. Instead, we see that the Sangha is our support. When we see a sister move in mindfulness, speaking with love, and enjoying her work, she is our reminder to return to our own source of mindfulness. Returning to mindfulness is to return to solitude.

When we enjoy our time with the people and friends around us and we don't feel lost in our interactions with others, then even in the midst of society, we can smile and breathe in peace, dwelling in the island of ourselves.

Source: http://plumvillage.org/mindfulness-practice/solitude/

About the Author

Phe X. Bach is a Buddhist practitioner and an educator in the greater Sacramento area. He is a husband and a father of two sons, residing in Sacramento, CA. He is an Instructional Leadership Corps professional development workshop trainer. He is teaching Mindfulness in the classroom for educators throughout California. Phe Bach acquired his Doctor of Education in Educational Leadership with a concentration in HRD at Drexel University. Dr. Bach is a Buddhist Practitioner and a Vietnamese Buddhist Youth (GDPT) leader. Currently, he teaches Chemistry at Mira Loma High; he also has been teaching Mindful Leadership and Mindfulness in the Classroom to educators in California since 2014.

He was born in Nhon Ly, Quy Nhon, Binh Dinh, Vietnam in 1976. In his early years, he finished 6th grade in Vietnam and started as a sophomore at Lincoln High School, Lincoln, NE. He got his Bachelor of Science, Biology; with minors: Chemistry/Psychology at the University of Nebraska, Lincoln, NE and got accepted into the PhD program in Bio-Organic Chemistry at UC Davis. After 4 years of studying graduate school, teaching and researching, he earned his Prof. Clear Single Subject Teaching Credential in Science with CLAD, University of California, Davis and teaches Chemistry at Mira Loma High since then. He also got his Preliminary Administrative Credential, CSU, Sacramento and a Master's Degree in Educational Leadership and Policy Studies, CSU, Sacramento. He earned his Doctoral degree in Education, Educational Leadership and Management at Drexel University, concentrated in Human Resources Development.

Phe writes as a way to preserve, promote and empower the Vietnamese language, culture and heritage while promoting the message of compassion, understanding, love, and mindfulness. He composes poems, writes articles and conduct research in English and Vietnamese on different websites and magazines both in Vietnam and in the USA. He is also presenting his research and sharing mindfulness throughout the United States of America, Thailand, and India. He also volunteers with the Buddhist Pathways Prison Project since 2011.

Qua Đi Qua Đi – Gate Gate Paragate

1.

Gió thổi vi vu	*Wind howls gently*
Trần gian nóng bức	*Hot and humid*
Phật cười thiên thu	*Buddha laughs eternally*

2.

Mưa rơi ướt ẩm	*The rain falls, humid and wet*
Sấm chớp	*Lightning and thunderstorm*
Có không	*Come and go*
Phong cầm ngân tiếng	*The wind chime sings*

3.

Mưa to qua đây	*The heavy rain just came by,*
Ướt bàn tay Phật	*Soaking Buddha's hands*
Long lanh chiều tà	*Glittering in the sunset*

4.

Bụi trần	*Life's dust*
Mưa quét	*Rain sweeps*
Sạch tâm	*Purify the heart and mind.*

Phe X. Bach, Ed.D.

Lightning Source UK Ltd.
Milton Keynes UK
UKHW020945160223
417123UK00007B/768